Yoga Sutra:
The 21st Century Worldview

Pradnya Dharmadhikari

Dedication

With deep gratitude to my parents

Tara and Raghunath Adke

who encouraged and supported, and in spirit still do, all my ventures in life

Copyright: 2020 Pradnya Dharmadhikari

Publisher: KDP Direct Publishing

Printed in the United States

ISBN: 9798606695959

Acknowledgments

This book would not have materialized without the support and cooperation of many of my Yoga asana co-practitioners and friends during the last several years. Katherine Frith, and Stephanie Dollinger provided suggestions that helped shape the organization of my arguments. Rosalba Correa, Ulrike Tragoudas, Luca Cruzat, Elizabeth Coelho, Marie McGlennen, Stephanie Dollinger, and Mariela Gomez, joined me in reading the commentary on the Sutras and frequently offered their thoughts. All these were instrumental in shaping and re-shaping my interpretations of the Yoga Sutra.

The motivation for writing this commentary came from observing the ease with which my growing grand-children, Sonali, Nilay, Alexandra, and Naviya, have gained expertise in navigating around the internet world. Experts in psychology and education have noted several important issues related to the immersion of the young and old in this new world of constant connectivity. Given that, it is imperative that the young and their parents become aware of those issues. This book, therefore, is for the growing citizens of the 21st century everywhere and for their friends, and all parents. Yoga asana practices are widely being adopted as a way of maintaining well-being everywhere in the world. Without an understanding of the concepts that provide the basis for those and the value for those practices, much is left out. Hopefully this book will provide some of that much needed understanding.

Last but not the least, I am grateful to my husband, Sudhakar, for being my sounding board and providing me the support throughout the process of writing this book.

———————

Contents

Preface

Yoga is an ancient Indian discipline that has its roots in spiritual practices that are more than 4000 years old. The development of a philosophy of yoga has been of an incremental nature. From appropriate breath work with chanting of ritual mantras and sitting positions, it gradually evolved as a comprehensive philosophy of life and provided ethical and practical guidelines for living. Its practices are based on a few philosophical concepts and directed towards self-understanding and understanding one's relationship to the world.

Yoga is one of the six Indian 'darshanas' that clarify some aspect of truth, with each having its own methodology. A 'darshana' represents a certain view, a certain perspective towards understanding reality. All 'darshanas' accept, to a certain degree, the authority of the Vedas, dated approximately between 2500 and 600 B.C. The 'darshana' philosophies are based on cold critical reasoning and analysis of knowledge. Poetry and religion are put aside. No single name can be attached to the philosophical concepts and meditational and other practices in Yoga until the end of the third millennium before present. Around the turn of the current era appeared the Yoga Sutra, a compilation of 195 two line aphorisms. The name Patanjali is associated with this compilation and, also with grammar (Mahabhashya). There is no definite historical information available about Patanjali. Apparently, he was also known as Govinda Yogi who had deep knowledge about all aspects of Yoga including its techniques.

The Patanjali Sutras are considered to have been written between the second century BCE and the fourth century CE. The philosophical arguments and concepts therein are based on an older Indian philosophical document, the Samkhya Karika. The philosophical arguments are meaningful and relevant for the modern world and the guidelines regarding ethics and personal disciplines are practical. The Gita (4.3) refers to the yoga tradition as ancient, age-old and yet ever fresh.

According to the Yoga philosophy while we are aware of the body and the mind, there are levels of awareness within that we remain unaware of. However, these deeper levels of awareness can be accessed and explored through the progressive process of introspection bringing about freedom from duhkha or suffering. The various meditational techniques are instrumental in providing such relief.

The Yoga Sutra focus is on life experience, primarily the suffering that is invariably associated with pursuing our inborn and acquired desires and aspirations. It analyzes and suggests ways of alleviating that suffering through various practices. While introspection based self-understanding is the primary focus, it is put in the context of how we relate to and interact with others within the setting of the larger human and material universe.

A 'sutra' (aphorism) is a brief statement of a principle. Each sutra has one or two lines and each line has no more than six to eight words. The essential meaning is presented in those few words, since there was more reliance on memory than on printed books. The concise presentations were passed on orally from generation to generation. Their brief form allows varied interpretations and there are many commentaries to facilitate understanding them. These continue throughout history and into the present.

There are four chapters in the Yoga Sutra compilation and each chapter has about 50 Sutras or aphorisms, except the fourth one which has 34. These describe and prescribe all the pertinent details of the yogic concepts and practices in a very concise manner. The Sutras do not provide elaborate instructions for the practitioner. Instead the focus is on letting the practitioner explore into the experience associated with each step under the guidance of a teacher.

Most extant commentaries on the Sutras focus on generally elucidating the philosophical concepts and the practices in this discipline. This book aims to provide an interpretation of the Sutras (aphorisms) from the point of view of addressing the problems that have emerged due to the wide-spread adoption of internet-based advances in communication. The concepts and practices are described with a view to suit the needs of the times. These can be a resource for teachers and young adults who are looking for an anchor in today's fast changing world. They are relevant and meaningful for the young and old in the modern world.

The world view that is the basis of the Yoga Sutra is time-tested. Its message is that we have the power to change things by changing ourselves. Existential ignorance can be weakened by calming the mind. Thoughts, feelings and emotions constantly occupy our minds and drive our behaviors. Memories and dreams about the future keep us from fully experiencing the present. Many conflicts are avoidable through understanding our own mind, through self-discipline, ethical behavior, and dedicated effort. The discipline of Yoga is centered on psychological and physiological practices aimed at achieving and maintaining a state of emotional stability. These are compatible with modern developments in a wide range of disciplines, such as, philosophy, physics, psychology, neurology, and therapeutic options.

In the following pages, chapter one lays the groundwork regarding the behavioral and psychological issues that have arisen in response to the pervasive involvement in modern internet based communication. Chapter two is about the specific areas where the Yoga practices can be instrumental in addressing those concerns. The commentaries on the Sutras in the four chapters in the Yoga Sutra follow in Chapters three through six. The last chapter presents concluding remarks.

———————

Chapter 1

The 21st Century

During the last 20-25 years, technology has advanced at a super-fast pace. The explosive growth of computer technology has brought the whole world under its sway. The 21st century inhabitants everywhere seem to be fully immersed in the internet-connected world. According to the International Telecommunications Union (ITU), a UN agency, more than half of humanity will soon have access to the internet. A report from the University of California, San Diego, says that in 28 years -- from 1980 to 2008 -- our consumption of information increased 350 percent, while our downtime continues to shrink. Staying connected is an addiction, raising dopamine, the feel-good chemical in the brain. One keeps looking for a fix, wherever available.

Oliver Sacks lamented that everything is in the public now. Anyone can be stocked with wide-ranging information but not necessarily have knowledge. The machine has taken over many aspects of our lives. There is the subtle draining-out of meaning, intimate contact, from our society and our culture.[1] At the stores, there are self-check-out lines, eliminating jobs and those short personal encounters with others. Mail order and home delivery services eliminate most person to person exchanges. Distance learning and working from home have caught on. On the other hand, tremendous opportunities for enhanced economic options have become available and those have helped open new ways of thinking. Science is flourishing. All these have not only changed work and leisure environments but, also generated various un-foreseen problems related to our everyday choices, how we learn, perceive ourselves, and deal with contemporary needs and issues, both as members of society, and as individuals.

According to a special report in the Economist, dated Jan.5th, 2019, addiction to screens seems to have become per-vasive. Smartphones are in use everywhere. The current genera-tion is also experiencing mental and physical health issues, fi-nancial crises, mass murders and shooter drills in kindergarten schools. Fake news has been used for smear campaigns in the Philippines, and rumors about kidnappings caused murders in India. In Myanmar Facebook has been misused to deepen the hatred of the Rohingya minority.

Increasing numbers are saying that they have no religion. These 'nones' will soon outnumber Catholics, Protestants, and evangelicals. However, God as an external entity is not replaced by inner convictions and timely guidelines that provide a founda-tion for and guide our actions while still providing a sense of ease and peace in routine existence. Tocqueville, the 19th century philosopher, said: When no authority exists in matters of religion, any more than in political matters, men soon become frightened in the face of unlimited independence.

There is a growing field of literature, see [2-9], focusing on the psychological, neurological, and spiritual implications of and options for dealing with these challenges. Researchers and sci-entists present opposing arguments regarding both positive and negative effects of digital media use. Among the negative effects, there are concerns about mental health of heavy users of social media and of video games. There is sleep deprivation, anxiety, depression, and cyber bullying. Playing violent video games results in aggressive thoughts and behaviors, and weakens prosocial behavior.

The following are some of the emerging problem areas, especially among growing children and young adults, that need to be attended to.

A. Hyper-stimulation, Reactivity.

B. Recurrent stress, Burnout.

C. Materialism, Consumerism.

D. Inability to sustain attention.

E. Weakened Interpersonal relationships.

F. Ego, Narcissism.

G. Existential angst.

Both the previous and current generations lack understanding regarding how to handle and cope with the challenges that the new experiences generate. The wide range of these issues, covering individual aspirations as well as socio-economic imperatives, necessitates our considering ever-changing biological, psychological, and philosophical issues related to lifestyle options. There is the ever-present tendency to find quick fixes, medications for problems such as ADHD, anxiety and depression. Reframing a situation, examining it from a different perspective, a new way of looking at one's own thinking and experiences, can help reduce certain anxieties and worries. Body/mind centered practices can provide opportunities for distancing oneself from routine anxieties and gain new insights about life. The concepts in Yoga provide a practical foundation for routine life. There are many practice options to choose from, options that are flexible and compatible with different life-styles. Plus, they can leave lasting benefits.

The New Connected World

The conflicting options and recurrent imbalances due to our thinking and the actions that follow them result in different forms of and degrees of dissatisfaction in life. They can be examined in the context of the following three things that we hold dear to us. These are:

1) We yearn to have a productive and well-integrated life as members of society.

    Here, among the problem areas listed above, the first three (A-C) are areas of concern.

2) It is important for us to establish, maintain and nurture our own separateness from others.

    This centers on the clash between individual aspirations vs. the security and comfort that belonging to the larger whole bring. Out of this emerge issues about identity, self-development, and inter-personal relationships. (D-F)

    And last, but not the least, is our need:

3) To be alone, and at peace with our options. This centers on the bigger questions about life, its nature and meaningfulness. (G).

Given below is a look at the problem areas that the 21st century generation faces and how certain Yoga concepts and practices can be used for dealing with them.

A.   <u>Hyper-stimulation, Reactivity.</u>

In today's internet-connected world, nonstop and finger-tip availability of entertainment and various distractions have become the norm. While these capture our attention, thoughts and reflection do not get attended to. Building long-term memory requires patience and thoughtfulness. We are in a rush to respond, comment and move on. Video games and watching TV not only affect sleep but also lead to decline in comprehension. The young are in a hurry to succeed and find the perfect job. But the fast pace of technological changes means changing demands for new skills.

Distance learning and long-distance working with others, is becoming more common. Work from home is also becoming common. These do not provide opportunities for learning from others, sharing life experiences, or forming strong work related alliances. For those who share the same work place, there arise periodically, stressful situations that cannot be avoided. One's own attitudes, habits and personality traits play a role in whether one reacts passively, aggressively, or cooperatively. Awareness about one's own reactive tendencies, whether one wants to be in control, or whether one tends to avoid confrontation, or whether one is more open to negotiation and trust, are some of the factors that are important in work situations. Passivity hurts the individual himself/herself, and so does wanting to exert control all the times. The result is frustration when one cannot respond or argue.

The ability to listen, as well as to communicate effectively play an important role in understanding other perspectives and in maintaining smooth connections. The reactive responses come from defending the ego and its needs. There is the 'me' and the 'other' and it brings out competition and conflict. Emotion-related triggers spread quickly. Sense-control and self-restraint, and ease with non-verbal communication, are crucial for advancing in any field.

Patanjali's Ashtanga Yoga emphasizes the importance of certain virtues. These are aimed at maintaining restraint and re-specting the other. These are followed by specific self-disciplines. There are breathing techniques that help cultivate restraint. These are crucial for self-understanding and learning to recon-sider before acting on any impulse. All these practices can help strengthen will-power and therefore are vital in curbing habitual impulsive responses. The body and breath related practices are also helpful in developing awareness about the senses and how to weaken their hold on the mind.

B.   Stress, Burnout:

Stress is widespread in the modern world. Everywhere there is emphasis on keeping busy. Everyone is running every-where looking for excitements, for opportunities to make money, find pleasures, meet people and visit places. This applies to all age groups. Children are busy playing computer games or doing social networking. Young adults are so busy that sleep depriva-tion has become a common problem. Working men and women are constantly on the run, from one chore to the next. There is no time to pause. Stress is insidious and damaging to the health of the body and the mind. A busy mind in hurry misunderstands, exaggerates, overlooks, and vacillates. It jumps to conclusions and rushes to judgment.

Burnout has become common because of 60+ hours work weeks, goaded by ambition, more money, and pushy employers.

In that process vitality is compromised, and connections in work and in life become lost. Depression and anxiety are issues affecting modern societies. Our thoughts and emotions are useful, guiding and energizing us; but unless some level of awareness is maintained, they have the potential for taking us off course, taking us into stressful situations. A continuous chatter of thoughts, of activities, is draining, and stressful. The dynamism of mental and material processes overwhelms us.

Refraining from "multitasking," giving our full attention to whatever we're doing, is part of training attention. Mental regeneration requires sense-control and self-examination. The connection between the body and the mind and the interactions between them cannot be overlooked and therefore, when it comes to stress-relief, both the body and the mind need to be enlisted. It helps to make space in our schedule and use that space to cultivate other interests, and build up energy reserves. While all effort is directed towards attaining a marketable skill, cultivation of hobbies is an activity that is often overlooked. Any activity that energizes, brings pleasure, is healing.

In everyday living the senses can be trained by choosing carefully what we eat, read, watch, and listen to. Ekanath Easwaran said: There is wisdom in slowing down. We need time for pondering life's deeper questions. We need time simply to be quiet now and then. There is an inner stillness which is healing, which makes us more sensitive and gives us an opportunity to see life. The simple practice of taking slow and deep breaths slows down the chatter of thoughts.[10] In the West, the self, equated with the mind, is expected to be in charge. The concept of the mind in Yoga philosophy is different. The mind is the instrument of the basic consciousness, the Self seated deep within us. This mind instrument consists of sense impressions, thoughts and feelings, memories, and interpretations thereof, plus the mental grooves created by set in patterns of behavior. All these can be examined and restructured in ways that help us to weaken negative and nurture positive ways of thinking and behaving that make life a meaningful experience.

In the very first chapter Patanjali states the importance of calming of thoughts, both through practice as well as through cultivating judicious selectivity. There are various introspective practices listed throughout the document. The Yoga Sutra is primarily a meditation focused discipline. Meditation is a multi-faceted attention nurturing technique. Introspection, mindfulness, meditative absorption are different forms of self-understanding that are crucial for maintaining balance and peace in life.

C. Ego, Narcissism:

As part of the growing up process we collect several stories that become part of who and what we are. We get so tangled up in these that we lose being in touch with who or what we really are. There is an instinctive urge to seek power and status, but in pursuance of those we feel anxiety regarding possible rejection, failure and loss of power. A life based around financial success, private life, family, relationships, still tends to feel unsatisfying.

An excessive interest in or admiration of oneself and one's physical appearance is narcissism. It is self-centeredness, involving a sense of entitlement, a lack of empathy, and a need for admiration from others. It can be a self-destructive way of making choices given the false or limited understanding of one's own needs. It is important to break the pattern of self-preoccupation and notice that others are out there and that our well-being depends on their well-being too.

The tendency to look at others as different, less, and dangerous creates a gulf between people. This is called narcissism of minor differences. It can lead to bullying; either on-line or overt. Isolating, and demeaning someone can make the perpetrators feel powerful and important. But these make the victims feel vulnerable and can cause suffering by creating intense anxiety, making them feeling deserted and depressed.

Judging, being suspicious about others' motives creates hostile work and social environment to the detriment of all. It stands in the way of work efficiency and ease in communication and sharing of ideas. Cooperation and attention to social justice are more likely to build strong relationships compared to self-assertion and competition. In today's world empathy, cooperation and partnership are important for building relationships. Trustworthiness and fairness matter, as much as, success in the business world.

The Western view emphasizes individuality, whereas, in the Eastern view everything is regarded as part of the bigger reality. While self-assertion is deemed to indicate strength in the West, the ability to get along is valued in the East. The focus on individualism can result in egocentrism. A strong ego is conducive to reactivity, narcissism, over-confidence. It strengthens hostile attitudes, and de-values others. It is also associated with the search for fluctuating and superficial pleasures. It needs to be countered by understanding that we are not masters of everything that we do. That keeps some openness in expectations and moderate responses to success as euphoria, or to failure as dis-appointment.

Excessive self-preoccupation can be disruptive. We define each other. Developing a healthy individuality is more than just attaining certain proficiencies. It is about developing a centered self, and that is not being self-centered; it is a self that is inclusive of the interests and aspirations of others. This means the ability to listen and to yield, to surrender at times. Communication is a two-way street. That means both talking to and listening to the other. Erickson[11] said that identity formation depends on both reflection and observation. It is a process that takes place on all levels of mental functioning. The individual judges himself in the light of what he perceives to be the way in which others judge him in comparison to themselves and to a typology significant to them.

In Yoga philosophy, our apparent self is deemed to be a changing composite of our choices in response to the constantly evolving circumstances and life experiences. But our real identity is simply the fundamental awareness within us, the Self or the spirit that reaches out to experience life. Introspection and self-understanding depend on the ability to separate the real Self from the experience. Self-understanding depends on the understand-ing of our ever-changing perceptions in relation to the dynamism of the circumstances affecting life. The ability to be alone and to reflect on one's emotions in private is important and needs to be cultivated. Asana and pranayama practices are effective in draw-ing the mind inwards. That helps in self-assessment while coun-tering the pull of the external distractions.

Patanjali's Yoga is more than a physical discipline. The Yogic view of identity, the ethical norms and personal disciplines that are part of this discipline, provide powerful arguments for addressing various cultural issues arising from the above-mentioned emerging trends in the contemporary mindset of young and old.

## D.	Materialism and Consumerism

The constant bombardment of advertisements and promotions feeds desires, creating new and reenergizing old thirsts. The thirst for acquiring things, and possessions has increased in response to the constant lures and ease of moving objects from distant parts of world. It has become easy to achieve Immediate gratification. As a result, materialism and consumerism are gaining speed everywhere and neither enhances the quality of life. Technologies such as e-mail and smartphones exacerbate impatience and anxiety.

The availability of many options means spending time in evaluating alternatives. Superfluous things become useful and useful things necessary. Another consequence of increased consumerism, besides disposal issues of unused and unusable items, is the problem of storage. Levitin[12] reports that when faced with clutter, the cortisol levels, especially in women, spike. Elevated cortisol levels can lead to cognitive impairment, fatigue and suppression of the body's immune system. Researchers at Princeton University found that people performed poorly on cognitive tasks when objects in their field of vision were in a disarray.[13]

Ear-phones have become ubiquitous, feeding non-stop information and entertainment. According to Michael Merzenick who is a pioneer in the study of brain plasticity, the entire auditory cortex of many children may now be rewired for noise in ways that have devastating implications for a host of language related cognitive functions.[14] Matthew Sanford said that when the consciousness is moved into technology one ceases to experience the body. The industrial and technological revolutions have meant that we move farther away from our bodies, and one cannot rely on the daily course of life to ensure a healthy connection between mind and the body.[15]

Obsessive-compulsive behaviors too are becoming more evident. Adolescence is a particularly stressful stage. Unhappiness is occurring at a younger age, from 29 in the 1970s to 14.5 in 2006. Technology may be the factor to be blamed for this change. The teenagers today communicate with their peers online and face to face communication is becoming infrequent. Feelings of entitlement and egocentrism along with the loss of close interpersonal relationships at home, at school result in isolation. At the same time, there is the compulsion to stay connected to others, to multitask, and one gets easily drawn to flashing screens. The lure of instant success, name and wealth is delivered non-stop and meaningfulness is sought in becoming the center of attention. Teens are stressed and lack sufficient sleep. New college graduates are facing disappointments, while they feel lost in the bigger world, making them question if the investment in education is worth the long hours, transient relationships, and uncertain opportunities to make a living.

Considering the global scale of material and technological resources, a life style based on acquisition of materials cannot provide durable satisfaction. A simple lifestyle means fewer distractions. The ethical norms and self-disciplines that are part of Patanjali discipline are about exercising self-control and cultivation of humility. Self-discipline out-predicts IQ for academic success by a factor of about 2. It is considered by some to be the queen of all virtues, and the strength that enables all other strengths.[16]   In today's world, our well-being depends on well-being of others elsewhere. We need will power for getting along with others and for overriding damaging impulses. Only with patience and self-restraint can we attain something. A sustained practice depends on commitment and the ability to withstand the lure of distractions. A committed practice strengthens will. In Patanjali's Yoga Sutra there are Sutras that highlight the process of change that is consistent with the theory of evolution. Understanding and evaluating the multiple dimensions of shifting energies in everything can help in getting a better understanding about the environment as well as for coping with the shifts in personal and interpersonal experiences.

E.   Inability to sustain attention.

We work at developing our talents and pursue interests, and aspire to become valuable contributors to the society. Making a living requires acquiring appropriate skills. Usually this means acquiring skills that bring material rewards while also providing a sense of satisfaction.

Responding to the rapidly evolving new technologies and changing economic structures means changing work conditions. But while knowledge, in general, has become more accessible in the recent years; the attention span has become short. A 2015 Microsoft report claimed that the average human attention span shrank from twelve seconds in 2000 to eight seconds in 2013. It is easier to take in, accept new information at the expense of taking a more discriminating and well-thought approach, and that takes time. When there is little true thinking and one tends to react with superficial attention there is little opportunity to think critically. Information from all over the planet keeps constantly pouring in and it keeps the minds of young and old completely engaged. At the same time, audio and video entertainments have become a pervasive part of the modern lifestyle but we pay only partial attention to those.

During the day, there are several simultaneously possible trains of thought. How does one focus on a few? That necessitates withdrawal of attention from some things and redirecting it effectively to the desired activity. Perception depends on intention and attention. Attention follows desire or will. When engaged in reading, listening or texting, one is likely to be in a state of continuous partial attention. Plus, excitement over an initial expression reduces the ability to detect what follows next and that results in attentional blink. One misses other incoming bits of information, and social and emotional cues.

Attention-deficit has become a common problem. During 1999-2006, over 75 percent of deaths among teens between the ages of twelve and nineteen were due to accidents (mostly vehicle accidents), homicide or suicide (The National Center for Health Statistics data brief 37, 2010). Insurers estimate that in busy urban areas most traffic accidents are due to pedestrians using smartphones. Due to computers and cell phones the ability to pay sustained attention needed for any learning is jeopardized. In today's world, the computer provides the whole story in a few minutes. Then who wants to take time to read a long article or a

200-page book? Even googling has a negative effect on memory. Multiple 'apps' are always there to encourage procrastination. In making a choice between homework and entertainment, the young are easily captured by the latter option, while the modern world demands more and more skills related to technology.[17]

To be able to learn, to assimilate and process information and knowledge, one needs to cultivate the ability to pay sustained attention. Our cognitive skills suffer without it. When attention is focused on something, one feels at peace, new connections are found, and creativity is enhanced. However, the art of concentration needs to be nurtured through practice. It takes a sustained effort to build up the ability to pay attention. One needs curiosity and a will to learn, while keeping distractions away. Catching oneself when not paying attention weakens the tendency of the mind to wander.

In Patanjali's Yoga there are several Sutras that provide important guidelines towards developing and maintaining progressively deeper levels of absorption. The variety of options and practices are a significant resource that is compatible with different temperaments and preferences.

F.   Weakened Interpersonal Relationships:

In today's world, widespread adoption of web-based modes of communication has facilitated staying connected with others who have common aspirations and needs. However, without opportunities for eye-to-eye contact, inter-personal relationships with outsiders tend to weaken quickly. The sense of being alone, not belonging, starts taking hold. Emotions and thinking are bodily processes and awareness and understanding of others depends on cultivating awareness regarding where one stands in relation to others. Our emotions and body movements are linked with the corresponding movements of the listener. It is important to be able to keep one's own thoughts and interests aside for understanding what the other person intends to communicate. It is about being a spectator of someone else's emotions and interests. It takes patience and self-restraint to absorb and pause before responding and that needs emotional and social intelligence. Empathy is sharing emotions of the other. It is a quality that helps us understand the fears and concerns of others. if one remains self-absorbed, focused on one's own problems and agendas, others get put aside.

Online friendships may seem intimate, yet, without face-to-face contact, there is no actual involvement. It seems that despite the ease of communication with others, the incidence of depression and loneliness in modern societies is increasing. The average age of suffering depression for the first time in developed countries is in the early teen years. Loneliness is related to limited social interactions. It leads to feeling disconnected from others, and from one's community. Homes have become larger and everyone spends more time alone, connected to the internet in different parts of the house. While opinions can be shared with thousands of people, there are fewer non-virtual friends. In all this one loses any sense of perspective. Who has time to talk to the neighbors and to share common concerns? The attachment to the screens, instead of giving comfort, is more likely to increase anxiety, and becomes more distracting.

We are built to respond powerfully in a face-to-face dialog, to the expressions and emotions of the person we are interacting with. Much is lost in distant exchanges of a few thoughts. There is no direct connection to the feelings, emotions, and deep-rooted thinking of the other. Over-emphasis on staying independent, reaching out for new opportunities at the cost of severing family ties, and giving up on maintaining closeness to family members, have meant increasing number of households with one person only. That means loss of the close-knit form of person-to-person contact and communication.

On-line immersion in the concerns of others, in any on-going events, is partial and superficial. We are connected to others through the choices we make and distant relationships lack the depth of face-to-face communication. On the positive side, web based networks are conducive to building one's own family, group of friends, and communities. But without face-to-face communication they tend to weaken soon. Relationships, if left un-nurtured, become fragile. Strong relationships play an important role in overall life-satisfaction.

Yoga practices can be both personal and communal. And there are opportunities in today's world for pursuing both. Communal situations present great opportunities for building relationships, for practicing ethical norms and self-disciplines. These can enhance self-discovery.

The remedy for feeling lonely lies in opting for solitude. Solitary and silent walks in natural surroundings are effective healers. Solitude is not being alone; it is putting distance between our self and what troubles us. Among the rewards of solitude is an enhanced opportunity for self-reflection. We understand ourselves better and this nurtures our capacity for relating with others. We get a greater understanding of who we are and what we want to be.[18]

To resolve interpersonal conflicts, empathy is needed. Empathy depends on reflective thinking. Reflective thinking helps us have a better understanding of others. Self-observation, being more open and receptive to others and their concerns, strengthen relationships. Introspection is not narcissistic self-involvement. It is self-examination without identifying with an emotion, or a thought. Body and breath awareness and meditative practices are powerful tools for that.

G.   Existential Dilemmas:

The waning influence of religion and close family connections has meant absent or weakened nurturing of interpersonal and social values. Conflicting options and recurrent imbalances in life raise levels of dissatisfaction. According to Christophe Andre: Happiness enlarges our vision of the world, whereas suffering shrinks our attentional focus.[19] Cultural preferences, disinterest in traditional ways of thinking, eagerness to fit in, questions about identity, and quest for meaningfulness are some of the factors behind the dissatisfaction the young adults are experiencing in today's world.

Young adults are more prone to be drawn into in-person and on-line persuasions by dogmatic and zealous cohorts. While concerns about what is happening elsewhere in the world has raised awareness about global responsibility, it has also become easy to isolate oneself from all the conflicts and problems elsewhere. One may question the meaningfulness of it all and look for the unchanging reality behind the constantly evolving changes in the world around us.

We are always seeking to understand our individual experience in relation to what the world experience appears to be.

Given that neither remains static, we are constantly looking for a balance between the two. Everything keeps changing, nothing remains fixed. Our likes and dislikes change and therefore, our choices. We believe that the world of our routine experiences is the world that matters and therefore worth holding on to. But can we?

Religions have been part of providing answers for such questions. The closeness of a well-knit group in traditional societies used to be comforting. But when there is a preference for staying unencumbered by cultural norms, nurturing an identity that separates us from others is valued, and since there are no stable relationships in this ever-changing world, one is likely to feel ungrounded. Social and environmental justice matter. David Bohm said: What we perceive depends on what we believe. Examining one's belief from not just personal or local perspectives but from a wider, trans-cultural and global perspective matters for maintaining the health and harmony within our small worlds.

What is ethical thinking and behaving? It is not just whether our choices are consistent with the social environment, in general, but also whether they further the interests of all. What are our responsibilities to others? It is important to understand the local and global implications of our thoughts and choices. It is about right and wrong behaviors. In the 21st century It is important to replace the terms 'I want' ,'I choose' and "I feel' by the phrase 'I ought.[20] According to Andy Clark, a philosopher and cognitive scientist at the University of Edinburgh, our life experiences construct what we expect and want to be true. By regularly entangling with a wide range of devices, we extend the mind into the world. The extended mind has ethical dimensions as well. Hurtful expressions, false representations, denigrating others, and using little restraint damage and destabilize relationships. Destroying the surroundings therefore can be as damaging as a bodily attack.[21]

The Yogic view of life in today's interconnected world can be valuable in developing awareness about the individual, local, and global scale implications of our various life activities. It can be an important part of seeking and understanding where life satisfaction resides. There is the ever-present issue of suffering and discontent in life. We are all subject to certain common limited ways of thinking that affect our actions.

Wisdom is knowledge through subjective experience. It is about how we interpret and evaluate any situation. That involves self-understanding and experience. Ignorance about reality, and self-centeredness, are the two primary causes that limit our understanding. In addition, the dominance of desires, aversions and fears means experiencing unending stress in life. Throughout the document Patanjali addresses all these issues and there are guidelines regarding various practices and the implications thereof.

References:

1.	Sacks Oliver, 2019. The Machine Stops. In the New Yorker, Feb. 8, pp. 28-9.

2.	Levitin Daniel J., 2014. The Organized Mind: Thinking Straight in the Age of Information Overload. Dutton.

3.	Turkle Sherry, 2011. Alone Together: Why We Expect More from Technology and Less from Each Other. Basic Books, A Member of the Perseus Books Group, New York.

4.   Twenge Jean M. 2017. iGen: Why Today's Super-Connected Kids Are Growing Up Less Rebellious, More Tolerant, Less Happy – and Completely Unprepared for Adulthood. Atria Books.

5.   Turkle Sherry, 2015. Reclaiming Conversation: The Power of Talk in a Digital Age. Penguin Press, New York.

6.   Twenge Jean M. 2014. Generation Me: Why Today's Young Americans are more confident, Assertive, Entitled – and More Miserable Than Ever Before. Atria paperback, New York.

7.   Levitin Daniel J., 2014. Cited above.

8.   Prochnik George, 2010. In Pursuit of Silence: Listening for Meaning in a World of Noise. Doubleday, New York.

9.   Richtel Matt, 2010. 'Growing Up Digital: Wired for Distraction.' In The New York Times, Nov. 21.

10.   Easwaran Eknath, 1994. Take Your Time, The Wisdom of Slowing Down: How to find Peace and Purpose in Your Life. Nilgiri Press.

11.   Erickson Erik H., 1968. Identity: Youth and Crisis. W.W. Norton and Co., New York.

12.   Levitin Daniel J., 2014. Cited above.

13.   Nir Eyal with Julie Li, 2019. Indistractable. BenBella Books Inc., Dallas, TX.

14.   Merzenich Michael, 'Growing Evidence of Brain Plasticity. http://www.ted.com/talks/ Feb.2004.

15.   Sanford Matthew, 2006. Waking: A Memoir of Trauma and Transcendence. Rodale Inc.

16. Seligman Martin E. P., 2011. Flourish: A Visionary New Understanding of Happiness and Well-Being. Free Press, New York NY.

17. Richtel Matt, 2010. Cited above.

18. Turkle Sherry, 2011 and 2015. Cited above.

19. Ricard Matthieu, Christophe Andre, and Alexandre Jollien, 2018. In Search of Wisdom: A Monk, a Philosopher, and a Psychiatrist on What Matters Most. Sounds True, Boulder, Colorado.

20. Sacks Jonathan, 2003, The Dignity of Difference: How to Avoid the Clash of Civilizations. Continuum, London, New York, NY.

21. MacFarquhar Larissa, 2018. Mind Expander. In the New Yorker, April 2, pp.62-73.

Chapter 2

The Yoga Worldview

The recurring argument in Yoga philosophy is that we have the power to change things by changing ourselves. Accordingly, the A-G problem areas discussed in the Introduction can be addressed through practices that nurture the ability to exercise restraint, develop listening skills, pay attention, and foster the sense of authentic identity. Thoughts, feelings and emotions constantly occupy our minds and drive our behaviors. Past happenings and anticipations of times ahead keep us from fully experiencing the present. Thoughts and impressions lead us towards acting on them but strength lies in resisting the pull of our conditioned way of reacting. Patience and restraint matter.

To address the various issues discussed in the earlier chapter, the following eight key concepts in the Yoga Sutras can be identified. Nurturing our understanding related to those concepts can be instrumental in enhancing our ability to deal with the needs of the times. These are:

1. <u>Attention</u>:

The inability to hold attention is the most important issue in modern life, and the next seven concepts have a direct bearing on that. As mentioned before, Patanjali's Yoga Sutra is primarily a meditation centered document. Patanjali not only understood how the mind works but also provided different ways of changing unhealthy mental patterns and establishing healthy ones. By developing sensitivity to incoming experiences and by consciously tuning into the inner dialogue, one can examine personal issues in different areas of life. That can bring in broader awareness. There is always some negative mind-chatter, but we can replace self-damaging thoughts by positive ones and engage in productive and creative activity. This enhances awareness and allows introspection. As a result, one is less reactive, and more receptive. The practice of meditation is a powerful tool. Systematically and steadfastly practiced, it trains the mind, sharpens the ability to pay attention and strengthens will. The habit of self-study that one learns to cultivate on Yoga-mats and meditation-cushions can be extended while doing routine chores.

2. Afflictions:

There are certain common ways of thinking that condition and limit our self-understanding and understanding of the world around us. The Sutras focus on five afflictions that are part of experiencing life and related to the level of satisfaction attained in it. These have implications in terms of actions and their effects, our aspirations, our ideas about identity and the nature of the world that we live in. Yoga practices can be instrumental in easing psychological tension and for the calming of the mind. It can also mean release of long-suppressed emotions. Suppressed emotions and feelings are obstacles to learning as well as for maintaining a certain ease in life.

Among the key concepts that provide the basis for the various practices enumerated in the Yoga Sutra is about the nature of reality. The Yoga system takes a dualistic view about reality. Purusha and Prakriti are the two basic and eternal realities that manifest in the form of diverse beings and diverse environments. First, the consciousness deep within us, is Purusha, the basic, receptive awareness, or the power of seeing and experiencing the world. And that is our soul, the spirit, or the true Self. Our awareness is like the surface of a mirror. It simply reflects. Nothing adheres to it. It simply remains receptive to our perceptions and emotions. Yoga philosophy considers it to be beginning-less and unchanging. Each Purusha is a separate individual, yet not separate from other Purushas.

3. Self:

The soul is referred to as 'atman' in Indian philosophy. The root term means breath, breath that makes a being. Knowledge about the Self involves knowledge and awareness about one's own body and about the workings of one's mind. Our present apparent self is the result of the past experiences, constantly evolving and subject to our choices. Its future form is in our hands. The yogic process of self-discovery starts with learning to observe the sensations in the body as it moves, and while it is in stillness, and the actions we choose to undertake.

4. Reality:

The Material World (Prakriti), is the counterpart of the awareness within us. It is beginning-less but subject to changes. Perceptions, feelings, emotions, thoughts, memories are all deemed to be   part of the material world. Everything material has inertia, an active energy, and an illuminative quality. These are described as qualities or energies ('Guna'). They are also interpreted as unconscious drives. We have the drive to move and act, and at times, the drive to withhold action. We also have the drive to engage in creative ventures. These three drives are held in a dynamic balance and respond to shifting conditions. We are at ease when the three are in balance and stressed without that. For material objects, such as wood or stones, imbalance brings about changes in form or function which we associate with the passing of time.

The function of the universe is to provide the world experience to the Self, the awareness deep within us. The universe is instrumental in providing right understanding regarding that experience, for freeing the mind of the afflictions, and for lifting the limitations on our perceptions and thoughts, that beset all beings. Our reality consists of our understanding of the evolving mental and material universe. We have the power to broaden that understanding and enhance our life experience.

5. <u>Mind</u>:

Yoga philosophy says that we are not our minds, or what our thoughts are. We exist beyond the level of the mind. The world is dynamic. There are shifting alliances and connections and these can jeopardize one's sense of identity. Following one's own aspirations, and strengthening the ability to carve out one's own course in life are values we all like to pursue. Yet selfishness and self-centeredness rarely produce positive results. The inability to exercise self-control and disregard of the growing inequities all around the world, sow seeds of conflict and hurts all.

Establishing healthy, benign behavior patterns matters. In our routine life, a random perception catches our attention and becomes a thought. The mind jumps from one to the next, rarely staying in place long enough to make sense out of it, or put it in any perspective in relation to anything else. Such shifts in attention mean loss of opportunity to take in a perception in all its different facets.

An important concept in Yoga psychology is that of 'Samskara'. A 'Samskara' is a thought, an action repeated over and over. It establishes a hold on the mind. The collection of 'samskaras', the patterns of our thoughts and actions make us what we are. Conditioned thoughts and repeated actions become powerful and sticky motivators that keep us moving in certain grooves. Yoga practices are geared towards strengthening only those grooves we wish to create and strengthen.

The primary means for altering any habitual ways of thinking and behaving is through the cultivation of the ability to sustain attention. For that it helps to take a systematic and progressive look at the inner realms of the mind. It is possible to eliminate the mental patterns that distract and bring life dissatisfaction. The power of the mind cannot be underestimated, a realization that is also gaining attention in the modern medical community. The meditative practices are an important part of restructuring our mental states.

6. <u>Ethics:</u>

Introspective understanding depends on following ethical norms and self-disciplines. Ethical virtues provide the foundation for a strong sense of identity that supersedes the narrow definitions of heritage and community. Following certain ethical norms is part of mental training. That means nurturing virtuous thoughts and behaviors and weakening tendencies that have disruptive effects. Value systems and ethics are not beyond science and technology. Our feelings of scarcity are related to our needs for peace of mind, love and leisure, community, and self-realization.

Norms, such as non-harming, exercising restraint, adhering to truthfulness, and containing greed, provide powerful arguments for addressing various cultural and environmental issues arising from the above-mentioned emerging trends in the contemporary mindset of young and old.

Yoga psychology acknowledges that our life satisfaction depends on how we relate to others. The relevance and importance of the implications of our choices in the local as well as the global settings necessitate exercising certain self-disciplines. Contentedness, humility, respect for the other, and honesty, ensure smooth relationships. This depends on whether we understand our own attitudes and whether we stay open to learning from others. Yoga provides various contemplative options that can provide satisfactory and feasible options in today's world. Many conflicts are avoidable though understanding our own mind, through self-discipline, ethical behavior, and having faith.

7. Practice:

The various practices involving the body, breathing, and meditation, are together conducive towards developing and strengthening introspection. The intellect, when refined, can observe the play of emotions and help to make decisions based on their value. Without such refinement, the tendency to react without giving much thought gains strength.

Attention-strengthening options include asana and breathing practices, refining attention, cultivating disciplined states of mind, concentrating and developing introspective awareness. The pace and depth of breathing changes in response to what type of thoughts are occupying our minds, mostly without our realizing it. The body responds in the same way and draws attention to the imprints of negative and positive thoughts that occupy our minds. The positive imprints are energizing and the negative ones limiting. When the body is held still and breathing is regulated, as in asana practice, the mind calms down. One can look at things from a different perspective. Introspection, looking inwards, plays an important part in coming to terms with the turbulent feelings and emotions that are frequently experienced during the adolescent years.

8. <u>Wisdom:</u>

Practice, dedication, and perseverance are important parts of this discipline. With perseverance in practice, the ability to examine all details of any object, or experience, to self-examine, is strengthened. This can provide a complete understanding of thoughts or experiences. Success in any venture depends on keeping one's psychic energies focused on appropriate choices. Creativity is enhanced when all the faculties are well-aligned and free of the constricting effect of discontent. It paves the way for knowledge and eventually for understanding life, and gaining wisdom that can address suffering that is part of living and experiencing the world. Wisdom is the ability to discern the real nature of a thing, the ability to tell the difference between the true and false. In Yoga philosophy, it means understanding the real nature of thoughts and experiences and their objects. And that is the ultimate objective of this discipline.

Patanjali's Yoga Sutra is a condensed document wherein the essential meaning is presented in few words. Those are simply pointers and it is left to the commentator to unravel the meaning therein. Various commentaries have been presented throughout history and into the present. A commentary on the Yoga Sutra that addresses the various above-mentioned issues that have emerged in today's world can fill in the need for practical corrective guidelines for today's young and old. Living introspectively, focusing on staying and savoring the moment, instead of constantly becoming or reaching out for something, can be learned. The practices help build connection between the body and the mind, and between the self and the community. The underlying concepts provide guidance with a clear goal as well as sound basis for a series of techniques that a practitioner can choose for reaching the desired goal. Being comfortable with who we are and with what others represent can deliver the inner peace that all seekers crave.

Hopefully, this commentary of the Sutras, highlighting the concepts and practices that Patanjali formulated, will help the reader and practitioner of the Yoga discipline to examine her own ways of thinking and practicing. The yogic way of distancing oneself and understanding the ever-changing experiences of life can help restore the balance that we yearn for. Through an intelligent and dedicated personalization of Patanjali's directions may you find balance and peace and in your life.

Chapter 3

I. Total Absorption (Samadhi)

The word 'samadhi' means settled (sama) mind or intellect (dhi). Accordingly, this chapter focuses on the settled state of meditative absorption. It defines Yoga and describes the different movements of the mind. It addresses a practitioner who has attained a certain degree of proficiency in the practice.

The first four Sutras are about what Yoga is.

<u>Introduction</u>

I.1.   Atha Yoga Anushasanam

अथ योग अनुशासनम् ।

atha: now; Yoga: union; anushasanam: presentation of rules and precepts

Here begins the instruction on Yoga.

This Sutra announces the subject of the teachings that follow. The term 'Atha' is used to indicate an auspicious beginning. This is the call to attention, and the importance of being present in the moment. It is usually invoked at the start of a discourse. Here, the discourse involves a detailed introduction and formal explanation of the discipline of Yoga. The use of the word 'atha' or now also suggests that the knowledge contained therein is old and is brought forth to the attention of disciples. It may also mean that it follows some earlier preparatory discourse. It is possible that it follows an earlier text on grammar about communication and comprehension, attributed to Patanjali.

Traditionally, the term Yoga has been variously defined. The scriptures speak of Yoga of devotion (Bhakti Yoga); Yoga of action (Karma Yoga); Yoga of Knowledge (Jnan Yoga); and Yoga of meditation (Dhyana Yoga). Here we focus on Dhyana Yoga. This Yoga is also known as Patanjali Yoga, or Raja Yoga. It can be described as; union of body and mind; harmonizing all levels of consciousness within; and is about individual consciousness and the objective world. Patanjali, the key figure associated with Dhyana Yoga, followed the extant knowledge of the role of the body and its health. He formulated the deeper psychological im-plications and philosophical background primarily based on the Sankhya 'Darshana', the oldest, and on the other 'darshanas' that evolved thereafter. Each 'darshana' presents and focuses on a specific worldview.

The term 'anushasanam' addresses the interested student to follow the Yoga discipline, which is a practice, subject to a set of rules, and has a disciplined code of conduct and precepts. The practices and concepts supporting them are presented here through the subsequent Sutras.

Key word: Attention

<u>What is Yoga?</u>

I.2   yogah chittavrtti nirodhah

योग: चित्त वृत्ति निरोध: ।

yogah: yoga; chitta: mind; vrtti: fluctuation, state; nirodhah: restraint, control

Yoga is establishing the mind (chitta) in stillness.

This Sutra represents the first important step in Patanjali's compilation. Patanjali describes Yoga as establishing the mind in stillness, free from any distractions. 'Chi' means to observe. The word Chitta, means 'seen, perceived' .'Chitta vrtti' means the selected parts of what has been observed. Seeing or perceiving is the domain of the mind complex consisting of the sensory mind, the interpretative faculty assigning meaning, and intelligence. The sensory mind connects with the material world, and the intelligence presents it to the Self or awareness. Like the material world the mind is changeable. The basic awareness itself, which is non-material; uses the material medium of the mind to connect with the world.

A thought, vrtti, represents a relatively superficial part of the mind complex and is about choosing to attend to a sensation, to a feeling or experience, sometimes momentarily and sometimes longer. Many thoughts mean connecting to multiple feelings and experiences. Most thoughts tend to be repetitive. They can be either wrong or questionable. Thinking comes in the way of fully experiencing the happening in that moment. It interferes with whatever one may be doing. Thoughts take us away from the present and to times and places somewhere else. They can be burdensome and cause stress. Thinking is speculating about reality. We describe things by assigning meaning to them that may not be what they truly are. This is reductionism and limits perception, creating problems in life. Intelligent and focused thinking enhances life experience.

The title of this first chapter is "Samadhi', which means integration, or pulling together of diverse strands. According to one interpretation of this Sutra, Yoga is the ability to direct and focus the mind on a single activity. Multiple thoughts pull us in different directions and interfere with our ability to concentrate. When actions and the resultant experiences pull us away from whatever we may be trying to pay attention to, conflicting thoughts arise, and we experience unease. The ability to concentrate indicates the ability to choose our thoughts. Direction entails examination, choice and following through by appropriate behaviors.

'Nirodha' is rejection, which means holding off, restraining, and is about how to deal with disturbance. This is a mental discipline that suggests that it is not through control but through redirection and selective attention that thoughts become constructive. Only then is their tendency to interfere with whatever we may be attending to is weakened. There is little willpower when the mind is engaged in various thoughts. The result is feeling unease and unbalanced. When there is attention, observation and non-attachment there is less chance of being pulled into automatic and reactive states.

Yoga means union, balance, and a harmonious state of mind. Having a mind that is free of the clamor of thoughts is needed for introspective understanding. The stilling of thoughts helps the mind to settle in silence. That silence is helpful in accessing and understanding one's own mental states and tendencies. A peaceful and quiet mind is indicative of harmony and an inner order, and the process of Yoga aims to establish that order. Its practices are directed towards developing the ability to direct and focus mental activity.

Understanding the mind, its limitations and the nature of its afflictions, helps connect the superficial aspect of one's being to the deeper inner layers of consciousness. William James aptly said: Our normal waking consciousness, rational consciousness as we call it, is but one special type of consciousness. Whilst all about it, parted from it by the filmiest of screens, there lie potential forms of consciousness entirely different.[1] The message of the Sutra above is that a human being is not what we think of as our mind, consisting of the sensory awareness and thought processes related to those. Nisargdatta[2], the modern Indian mystic said: What you are, you already are. By knowing what you are not, you distance that from yourself. You are the pure awareness that illumines consciousness (the mind complex and its infinite content). We exist beyond the level of the superficial mind, and beyond our thoughts. We need to delve deep into the mind and its stirrings.

Descartes said: "I think, therefore I am." Modern scientific studies tell us: "I am; therefore, I think." And calming of thoughts is the beginning of that process of finding the 'I'.

Key words: Attention, Self, Mind, Practice

1.   James William, 2004. The Varieties of Religious Experience. Barnes and Noble Classics, New York

2.   Nisargadatta Maharaj, Maurice Frydman and Sudhakar S. Dikshit, 1973. I Am That: Talks with Sri Nisargadatta Maharaj. The Acorn Press, Durham, North Carolina.

<u>What is the 'seer'?</u>

I.3   tada drastuh svarupe avasthanam

तदा द्रष्टु: स्वरूपे वस्थानम् ।

tada: then; drastuh: the seer; svarupe: In his state; avasthanam: resides

When that is accomplished, the seer rests in its existential identity.

When the mind is settled in silence, the 'seer' within us comes to the forefront. The 'seer', the seeing, perceiving entity within us, is the energizing principle, awareness, the ability to see, sense, and experience the world around us. It is also referred to as the Self, and is called Purusha in Yoga philosophy. The word Purusha literally means man. It can be more appropriately described as a 'being'.

'Seeing' does not simply mean seeing with eyes only. It means experiencing, cognizing the tangible and intangible aspects of our world. That world is described in Yoga as 'Prakriti' (meaning Nature). Purusha and Prakriti represent two complimentary aspects of reality. Without the other neither has any meaning. Purusha represents consciousness, an energy, and is about cognition and is subjective. On the other hand, objects and the mind are both cognized by Purusha. The qualities of these two are different.

There can be no consciousness without awareness, but there can be awareness without consciousness, as in deep sleep. Awareness is absolute, consciousness is relative to its content; consciousness is always of something. Consciousness is partial and changeful, awareness is total, changeless, calm and silent.[1]

We consider our awareness, beingness, to be our mind. But the mind is simply the instrument for the awareness; for experiencing the world, or Prakriti. This instrument, normally, provides an unclear and limited picture of the world to us. Only when the mind is stilled, and is stripped of its limitations and colorings, can it see the world as it is, and convey it that way to the seer. A mind in stillness tends to be free of distractions, unencumbered by narrow ways of thinking, and the perceptions are unmodified. In that state, previous experiences, or the past, do not interfere or color what is being observed, or experienced, in the present. Such unmodified information then allows the awareness (Purusha) within to maintain its true essence.

Purusha is 'drastuh' which means that which can see itself in the clear mirror of the mind. Awareness is a higher level of consciousness, unaffected and completely at ease and clear of any conditioned perception of the material world. Awareness is pure observation, pure seeing. What is pure seeing? Krishnamurti said: Looking at a tree without knowing anything about it, is pure seeing. But when one thinks of it as, for example, a maple or an oak, it is the image, the concept that is in front of us. Awareness can also perceive itself and everything inside and outside of us.

The information that the senses deliver tends to be more than we can absorb. Therefore, we select bits that support our beliefs and our world-view and leave the remaining part unacknowledged. This selectivity is a form of organization that helps us navigate our activities more efficiently while interacting with others. There are still times and situations in life when we need to take a comprehensive view of things, of all the interconnections and interdependencies, and their various implications. It is at such times that the ability to see things as they are becomes very important. And the Yoga discipline is valuable for developing that skill.

Key words: Reality, Self

1.   Nisargadatta Maharaj, Maurice Frydman and Sudhakar S. Dikshit, 1973. I Am That: Talks with Sri Nisargadatta Maharaj. The Acorn Press, Durham.

The mind is not the 'Self'

I.4   vritti sarupyam itaratra

वृत्ति सारूप्यम् इतरत्र ।

vritti: modifications of mind; sarupyam: Identification; itaratra: elsewhere

Caught in the changing states (of mind), we forget our true Self.

What is our true Self? Our Self or real identity is separate from the mind, intelligence, and ego. It is, the Yoga philosophy says, the deep-seated consciousness. It is the seeing light, the witness.[1] We, the 'seers', the knowers, are beings that have the ability of becoming aware of everything around us and that is what we are. The Self in Yoga is simply awareness and that is its essence or true nature.

The senses and the mind are for witnessing and experiencing the world around. Whatever the senses deliver, the sights, smells, feels and tastes, and whatever interpretation the mind puts to these experiences, all these are for presenting to our Self.

When our focus is on perceptions and thoughts we mistakenly take these to be those of our basic Self. The mind experiences anxieties, frustrations, and disappointments. Our perceptions are not always clear and true. When the mind is not still and is in the sway of distracting sensations and thoughts, it is like a wind-swept lake surface. Just like the waves that obstruct the view of the deeper reaches of the lake, the mind presents an unclear picture of its object of perception to our Self.

All our impressions and thoughts become part of our conscious memory, some are sequestered in the subconscious and some into the unconscious. This mind complex is a constantly evolving process, and does not represent our true Self. Its purpose is to present the world experiences to our true Self. Our basic consciousness, which is the true Self, the observing energy, or awareness itself, is a receiver of what the mind delivers.

Key words: Mind, Self

1.   Hiriyanna M., 1948. The Essentials of Indian Philosophy. Motilal Banarsidass Publishers, Delhi, India.

Sutras 5 through 11 describe the different thoughts that commonly occupy the mind.

<u>Thoughts; benign, harmful, or neutral</u>

I.5   vrttayah pancatayyah klishta aklishtah

वृत्तय: पंचतय्य: क्लिष्ट अक्लिष्ट: ।

vrttayah: thoughts; pancatayyah: fivefold; klishta: afflicted; aklishtah: unafflicted

Thoughts are five-fold. They may be cognizable, non-cognizable, painful, not painful, or pleasing.

All thoughts, feelings and mental states that grab our attention and need calming as part of the Yogic discipline can be classified into five categories, and are described in the following Sutras. We are either aware or unaware of their nature. Some stay latent and emerge later.

Some thoughts cause pain, are afflicted, and are called 'klishta'. These limit our understanding and negatively affect our actions. There are impulsive emotions and sometimes we are unable to accurately read a situation. Even positive emotions, such as, pride and self-satisfaction can be toxic if they make us insensitive to the concerns of others. Emotions like fear frequently result in impulsiveness, reactivity. These affect our ability to respond and behave appropriately. They usually mean our not correctly interpreting a situation. They can arise from the desire to protect oneself. Objectivity is lost when emotions grab the mind. On the other hand, when examined, even painful experiences can be enlightening and eventually beneficial.

Some thoughts bring pleasure, delight, enhance our understanding, increase creativity, and are referred to as 'aklishta'. Positive emotions, such as pleasure, empathy, friendliness, are more amenable to our thinking. They are more likely to be due to a realistic way of seeing. We are normally at peace, unless and until something happens to disturb that peace. Yoga practices are aimed at returning to such moments, either by addressing the cause/s for such disturbances or by moving away from them. Interestingly, we cannot hold two opposite thoughts in mind at the same time. The idea is to make it a habit of returning to positive thoughts.

Some thoughts are neutral (as when we look at a passing car). Like high clouds that are moving in the sky, they pass without interrupting the chain of thoughts occupying the mind. The quality as well as the number of thoughts matters and they affect our wellbeing in different ways. The body and the mind respond positively or negatively to most of our thoughts as they materialize in the form of our choices.

Key words: Afflictions, Attention, Mind

<u>Types of thoughts</u>

I.6   pramana viparyaya vikalpa nidra smrtayah

प्रमाण विपर्याय विकल्प निद्रा स्मृतय: ।

pramana: valid knowledge; viparyaya: misconception; vikalpa: imagination; nidra: sleep; smrtayah: memory

Thought types are true knowledge, false knowledge, imagination, sleep, and memory.

Yoga psychology considers five different kinds of thoughts. These are: thoughts due to right knowledge ('pramana'), error ('viparyaya'), imagination ('vikalpa'), sleep ('nidra'), and memory ('smriti').

The first two, 'pramana' and 'viparyaya', are based on direct contact with the world through the sense organs. The sense organs are under our control and through that control we think that we can directly connect with the world around us and experience the here and now. Yet, how often do we really connect with what we see and feel? Usually our senses provide right information, but sometimes they can mislead us. Sometimes we misinterpret what a sense organ delivers, such as, mistaking a snake for a rope. Human mind is a messy place with information flowing in from all directions, from distant places, and there is room for error at every step. More about these two types of thoughts in the following two sutras.

Inattention and distractions result in missed or misinterpreted details. Most of the times we remain caught up in the desires and fears that lead us to think of things that may or may be real. Imagining them to be there is 'vikalpa', which separates us from the actual; immersing us in the mirage of an alternative reality.

Sleep is a form of distraction for the mind. During sleep while one is unaware, one remains variously connected to the external world. In the dreams, there are combinations of sense based ('pramana'), misperceived ('viparyaya') and imagined (vikalpa) worlds. There can be absurd and random combinations of events and desires.

A memory is an imprint of an experience. Memory is indispensable for advancing in life and it can also be a block. Repeated thoughts and actions is like memorizing something and we tend to retain their import and they shape our minds.

All these five types of thoughts are world-connected states. They occupy our minds and are superficial, and ever changing in nature. When we are awake and present to the now we cannot resist remembering the past or anticipating the future. Thinking means overlooking what we may be engaged in. Each new thought modifies our previously held perception, leading to action. For being present to the here and now, for giving complete attention, requires preparation through examination, choosing and following through. And that depends on having an undistracted and calm mind. Whatever we recognize can be handled through practice and appropriate restraint. Many unrecognizable pains can be deferred through resisting the pull of distractions from far and near.

Key words: Attention, Mind

Sutras 7 through 11 describe the above-mentioned five thought types.

<u>What is valid knowledge?</u>

I.7   pratyaksha anumana agamah pramanani

प्रत्यक्ष अनुमान आगमा: प्रमाणानि ।

pratyaksha: direct perception; anumana: inference; agamah: word of authority; pramanani: proof

There are three kinds of valid knowledge: direct sense knowledge, inferential or logic-based knowledge, and knowledge based on reliable testimony.

Accurate and verifiable knowledge provides correct information about objective reality. Such information and insightful perceptions can be liberating, and calming. One's own direct sense-perception is instrumental for this purpose. The five senses provide information that the sixth sense, the mind, interprets. As has been said: 'The eye looks and the mind sees, the ear hears and the mind listens.'[1]

Inferences drawn from sense-perception are valid, such as when there is smoke seen, one can correctly infer that there is fire associated with it. These are based on observed regularities in occurrences.

Just as self-witnessed, self-experienced knowledge is usually correct, so is knowledge received from a trusted or reliable source. Verbal/written testimony from a reliable source can convey correct knowledge too.

While there are these three above-mentioned ways of receiving correct knowledge, that received through direct sense perception, compared to inferences and verbal/written testimony, is considered superior most of the time, since it is based on personal experience.

Inferences and words of authority are indirect ways of getting information, although they may be based on direct sense-perception. Substantiation of any such acquired information implies repeatability as well as concordance with reason and past experiences. In all these forms of valid knowledge, direct and indirect, it is the mind that remains the primary meaning maker. For that the mind relies on previous perceptions. New ways of thinking and technological developments modify convention based interpretations. In the modern internet-connected world sight and sound based information seem to have gained an upper hand over other sensory perceptions.

Key word: Mind

1. McCallum Ian, 2005. Ecological Intelligence: Rediscovering Our-selves in Nature. Africa Geographic, Cape Town, South Africa.

<u>What is misperception?</u>

I.8 viparyayah mithya jnanam atad rupa pratistham

विपर्याय मिथ्या ज्ञानम् अतद् रूप प्रतिष्ठम् ।

viparyayah: delusion; mithya: erroneous; jnanam: knowledge; atad: not in its own; rupa: form; pratistham: based

Viparyaya is false or illusionary knowledge based on things having no existence in fact.

Knowledge that is transmitted, received or interpreted wrongly is false. The senses themselves can cause incorrect perception. Stress can distort impressions, and thoughts based on those can mislead, despite their having arisen from direct observation.

When we do not completely attend to what we may be experiencing, it is negligence and that results in misperception. Multi-tasking results in partial attention. And excitement over an initial impression reduces the ability to detect what follows next, resulting in attentional blink.

The word 'viparyaya' literally means 'to flow away, or around'. It is information that is away from reality. It takes the form of misperception or some distortion of reality. A mirage, mistaking a rope for a snake, are examples. The actual condition, or nature of the object is revealed only under appropriate conditions. Labels for people, such as, Americans, Christians, Buddhists, or Hindus; can be misleading. These are sometimes useful, when they are used to identify a certain property, but they can also be harmful and, misrepresent reality by categorizing groups as homogenous entities. Misperceptions are also due to ignorance, egoism, preferences and aversions, and clinging to certain beliefs. Incorrect information is always there and one can get caught up in its flow.

Key words: Attention, Afflictions, Reality

<u>Imagination, Fancy.</u>

I.9   sabda jnana anupati vastusunyoh vikalpah

शब्द ज्ञान अनुपाती वस्तुशून्यो विकल्प: ।

sabda: word; jnana: knowledge; anupati: followed in sequence; vastusunyoh: devoid of meaning; vikalpah: verbal proficiency

'Vikalpa' is knowledge that is imagined and based on verbal proficiency.

Day-dreaming, abstract thinking, are examples of imagination. Knowledge that does not have any substantive basis is vague and uncertain. We use words to convey some meaning. However, they are simply representations. Plus, they do not completely describe the whole reality behind them. They are for identifying and high-lighting selected experiences and materials that we come across. The words God, religion, or identity do not represent anything that is real. Instead they create certain impressions in our mind and we hold on to those impressions, using our own inclinations, memories, experiences, and language; creatively. Nations, money, human rights, laws, justice are all vague terms and represent imagined realities.

Imaginations are based on sense-based perceptions and memories, although these are combined and recombined without any order and at times by using will. Described as conceptualization, these can create negative and narrow images based on limited criteria. Watching a movie, reading a book create images in our minds although many times they are not too far from what we have experienced in life.

Imagined experiences either keep us in the past or take our minds into the future. In both cases the present is left unattended. Imagined thoughts and experiences not only separate us from the real, those also help us create our own realities. Labels are an example of this. They do not necessarily represent reality. Our imagined reality becomes subjective, unlike the shared understanding, as in the case of sense based knowledge. Imagined disasters can agitate, and feelings of self-importance can lead one to building castles in air. Words, fanciful thoughts, fail to capture the whole reality. At the same time, we hold on to those as if they stand for something real and sometimes help us find escape from reality. We also carry misperceptions about our own desires and deep seated thought patterns. These can hinder us from finding genuinely satisfying options.

Imagination, and conceptualization, however, are useful as they help further the search for factual knowledge and discovery. For making life more bearable, for creating new worlds, the right use of imagination is needed. Certain experiences, such as thought-free total absorption ('nirvichara' Samadhi), cannot be described in words and are only known through subjective experience.

Key word: Mind

Deep Sleep

I.10   abhava pratyaya alambana vrttih nidra

अभाव प्रत्यय आलंबना वृत्तिर्निद्रा ।

abhava: absence of awareness; pratyaya: understanding; alambana: foundation, support; vrttih: thought-wave; nidra: deep sleep

Sleep is the non-deliberate absence of thought waves or knowledge.

In the dreamless state of deep sleep, the mind is at rest, and the senses of perception are quiet. We stay unaware of any conscious activity, but we are not unconscious. The conscious mind withdraws completely, while thoughts keep moving and there are no mental images. Deep sleep is blissful and we have no awareness of our separate existence. There are no felt experiences of the wakeful state. Since there are no perceptions there is no memory formation. The brain remains active even in deep sleep but does not acknowledge any mental activity, as it does when we are awake. However, absence of thoughts does not mean a totally inactive mind. Without any awareness on our part, the mind does stay engaged in other activities, such as finding answers, reactivating distant memories, and energizing desires.

After waking up one becomes aware of whether one has slept well or not. Depending on the quality of energy, serene, active, or dull; one feels rested, agitated or lethargic, respectively. If serene energy has prevailed one feels rejuvenated; like the rest and rejuvenation that occurs in deep meditative states. The happiness in deep sleep arises out of a sense of peace and wellbeing and is different from the temporary comfort that is due to physical pleasures. Modern research also suggests that in this state the autonomic nervous system is repaired. (Also see Sutra I.38)

Key word: Mind

<u>Memories</u>

I.11   anubhuta-visaya-asampramosah smritih

अनूभूत विषय असंप्रमोष: स्मृति: ।

anubhuta: experienced; visaya: object; asampramosah:
not letting go away; smriti; memory

Memory is holding on to past experiences.

Past experiences stay in our mind as memories. Memories can be based on actual as well as imagined experiences. Some impressions are of a fleeting nature, while some persist and become memories. A memory represents a past impression of both an object and how one perceived it then. The body, too, remembers sensations and learned movements. Useful for understanding and planning, memories can also limit and color and thereby change new experiences. With attention and conscious re-direction these can be rendered ineffective.

Stress, beliefs and judgments can limit perception and thus limit what is retained as memory. Some memories, especially those related to repeated or similar experiences get a foothold in the subconscious and become subsequent motivating tendencies, called the 'samskara'. Experiences leave impressions that either retain their hold through prejudicial assessment of the present or provide guidelines for choosing options in the future.

Most of our memories tend to be reconstructions of actual experiences. When we retrieve one, the brain rewrites it a little, updating it in the context of current concerns and understanding. The next time we bring it up we get the last, updated version. When a memory is recalled one gets a limited version of the actual experience. A memory is true when it represents the unmodified actual experience. Memories push us back into the past whereas the future pulls us in the opposite direction.

Key word: Mind

Sutras 12-16 focus on calming the mind.

Practice and Detachment

I.12   abhyasa vairagyabhyam tannirodhah

अभ्यास वैराग्याभ्याम तन्निरोध: ।

abhyasa: repeated practice; vairagyabhyam: detachment; tannirodhah: their restraint

Practice and detachment are the means to still the movements of consciousness.

The word 'abhyasa' is derived from abhi+as. The term abhyasa comes from the root 'abhi' for toward, to, unto, and 'asa' for seat, a stable position. Here it means the practice of yoga done with perseverance and without interruption. In Yoga, the objective is to calm down the thinking mind, and the various Yoga practices are aimed at helping channel attention. It is important to develop the mental strength for staying focused and detach oneself from the pulls of distractions. Success in this depends on sustained practice. A sustained practice depends on the support of appropriate choice for focusing while also maintaining an environment that is conducive towards staying with the focus of attention.

Detachment is not easy and like a muscle it needs to be strengthened through repeated use. Becoming aware that the mind is wandering is the first stage. Next, withholding the tendency to follow its object, or acting on whatever the mind demands. It takes repeated practice to keep the distance from what the mind demands. By not reacting to any distracting impulse, it releases energies from unneeded occupations and these can be focused on sustaining attention.

Overcoming old tendencies is also important for establishing the desired changes. 'Vairagya', or non-attachment to older options is the ability to look at thoughts as a spectator. Forceful suppression of desires, resisting with determination are indicators of ego and self-centeredness, not Yoga. Refraining from experiencing life is not advisable. It can make one emotionally unresponsive. What is needed is a progressive loosening of mundane attachments so that one can pursue the desired objective. A relaxed approach depends on understanding desires and fears and by not succumbing to distracting options. One can persevere in spiritual practice, 'abhyasa', while also nurturing joyous, friendly, compassionate and kind inclinations.

Key words: Attention, Practice

<u>Sustained practice</u>

I.13   tatra sthitau yatna abhyasah

तत्र स्थितौ यत्न अभ्यास: ।

tatra: in that case; sthitau: for stability; yatna: continuous effort; abhyasah: practice

A sustained practice is needed to still the mind's movements.

The objective in Yoga is to have a tranquil mind. In the present Sutra, Patanjali focuses on the importance of practice for attaining that. Developing a personal practice involves setting up and following a routine, and staying on the path. A continuing investment of time is crucial. A sustained practice means maintaining strong intention and focused attention. When the motivation comes from within and not because of some external urging, one is more likely to stay with the practice. Patanjali points to the long time it can take for calming of thoughts; and one needs to stay on the path patiently and persistently. Unless there is dedication, one is likely to be drawn off-course.

An attentive attitude and a mind free of any preconceived ideas is important. Focused attention is transformative and can lead to new insights and enhance creativity. Distractions should be kept at bay. One needs to recognize, and remove obstacles as and when they arise. Awareness about the benefits as they appear energizes the practice and one is less likely to feel disappointed and thus rebel.

An effective practice is pleasing and reassuring. Sometimes the effort seems to be too much but as one persists and as one experiences the benefits of a new behavior-pattern, the balance can tip in favor of continuing the approach and weaken any tendency to put off or to avoid practice. The desired results appear slowly and sometimes unexpectedly but they certainly do. A good practice, whether physical, mental or spiritual, empowers and expands the mind. It is respectful of any day-to-day differences, and more peaceful. Self-discipline in all matters needs to be habitual and, therefore, is crucial.

Key words: Attention, Practice

Practice with humility and without breaks

1.14   sa tu dirgha-kala-nairyantarya satkara sevitah drdha-
bhumih

स तु दीर्घ काल नैरन्तर्य सत्कार सेविता: द्रढभूमि: ।

sa: that; tu: indeed; dirgha: long; kala: time; nairyantarya: uninterrupted; satkara: right fashion, reverent devotion; asevitah: cultivated; drdha: firm; bhumih: ground

Long, uninterrupted practice with devotion is the firm foundation for calming thoughts.

Satkara also means attentive practice. A sustained regular practice over a long time is crucial for calming thoughts. Without it one does not feel any improvement. Distractions and discomforts tend to intervene and the practitioner needs to persist and keep up with the effort. Too much zeal and effort, passion are counter-productive. The Mundaka Upanishad suggests one needs to exert with energy, but with humility and without any pride. The more enthusiasm there is for practicing and the more effort one puts into it, the harder it is to keep up the desired effort. On the other hand, sincerity and singlemindedness strengthen the pursuit.

Meditation, for example, can be an intimidating practice for any novice. There are always obstacles when one wants to concentrate. For persons who are normally busy it may seem as a waste of time. There is a constant chatter of distracting thoughts, sensations and emotions. One may feel that the energies are getting scattered and dissipated. One can experience doubt about whether one can concentrate and meditate and that brings tension. There is also boredom, especially in the initial stages. An attitude of trust and devotion to the discipline is helpful at such times. Patanjali's advice is to keep on practicing for a long time without interruption. Carelessness and complacency can intervene if the will to continue weakens.

The ability to withstand the pull of alternative interests and priorities, of other objects of excitement, is as important as practicing on a regular basis. In any practice done with awareness, appropriate restraint is crucial. One should keep on returning to the practice until it becomes effortless. That gives the feeling of having established a firm ground of undisturbed calmness. In this state, there is neither any strain nor any resistance. Thoughts come and go and one simply observes.

Key words: Attention, Practice

Non-attachment

I.15   drsta anusravika visaya vitrsnasya vasikara samjna
vairagyam

दृष्ट आनुश्रविक विषय वित्रुष्णस्य वशीकार संज्ञा वैराग्यम् ।

drsta: seen, perceptible; anusravika: heard; visaya: object;
vitrsnasya: freedom from desire; vasikara: under control,
mastery; samjna: understanding; vairagyam: detachment

Non-attachment is the freedom from craving for all objects of desire, known or anticipated.

'Vairagya' (from 'raga' meaning attachment) is not getting caught up in responding to stimuli as they arise. It means attending to desires by first becoming aware of the bodily responses, evaluating them and then choosing to opt out of satisfying them.

Detaching from repeated experiences of desires and disappointments is the practice of renunciation. By being selective about which stimulus to react to, which stimulus to let go, we remain in charge of what we experience. The more we practice such selectivity the more mental strength we build up for resisting unwanted pulls. Once the pull of desires is overcome, we can choose to focus on what we really want. Patanjali says that when one feels no pull towards whatever one is dealing with or encounters, one can say one has achieved non-reaction. It is only then that one can clearly see, and have an undistorted experience of the world.

When a multitude of desires pull us in all different directions we feel stressed. When a desire is satisfied, we feel happy for some time. Yet that feeling soon passes and we crave for a similar experience. We get caught in the cycle of wanting and seeking satisfaction. A dependency develops. If satisfaction is not found we feel deprived and we do not like to experience disappointment. Recurrent cravings and disappointments are unsettling. On the other hand, when there is no craving there is no disappointment.

Yoga is about experiencing the here and now and not about what one may have experienced in the past or may experience in the future. For that it is important to have the will to stay unmoved by any craving or temptation. This does not mean that one suppresses desires. There are things in life that bring genuine satisfaction, such as, having a satisfying job, a child, a comfortable home. At the same time, it is up to us to decide how much effort we can put in having those without jeopardizing our ability to live in balance, at ease with our capabilities and limitations. Sooner or later one learns that desires do not remain intense for long nor do they last.

Key words: Afflictions, Attention, Practice

<u>Liberating effect of non-attachment</u>

I.16   tatparam purusha khyaterguna-vaitrsnyam

तत्परम् पुरुष ख्यातेर्गुण वैत्रुष्ण्यम् ।

tatparam: supreme; purusha: self; khyatair: vision; guna-vaitrsnyam: indifference to the energies of nature

When non-attachment becomes a way of life, one is liberated from the energies of nature and possesses the knowledge of the spiritual being that one is.

Our normal perceptions tend to be limited and mental clarity is not always present. We take the ever-changing conditions to be real and permanent. Our responses to those are driven by our insecurities, attachments and aversions. Non-attachment allows us to weaken the hold of these on us and instead focus on the experience within. It helps us to understand our emotional states. It also gives us the opportunity to become aware of the repercussions of our thoughts, words and actions. It is important to respond freely and deliberately, to take considered action, rather than engage in continuous reactivity. Ignorance about the real nature of reality is removed when we can delve deeper into the mind.

Our lives tend to be under the sway of three dominant qualities, energies, or tendencies ('guna') in us and in all objects. The balance of strength among these qualities keeps shifting in response to our urges or the circumstances. These qualities are illuminative ('sattva'), active ('rajas'), and inactive ('tamas'). The active and inactive qualities influence the perceiver, resulting in either action, or inaction, respectively. When there is detachment the wisdom oriented illuminative quality is strengthened. This helps disengage from the senses, and strengthens the ability to withstand the pull of desire. This stills the mind, and thereby weakens the active and inactive qualities.

When the mind is free of anxiety and fear, we are beyond thoughts of what is next, or what we need, or what needs to change, and we see the world fully and completely, and that is the superior vision that this sutra refers to. Seeing means becoming aware. Self-examination helps gain mental clarity. When the mind is silent, the intelligence within us helps us to see and experience things as they are, free of added interpretations. And that is when we get to know our real, peaceful and contented Self.

A spiritually enlightened person is one who has attained a complete, supreme, state of detachment. Things and experiences happen but they do not leave any impressions and when one remains above their pull there is no reactive movement. It is self-mastery. When the deeper levels of consciousness are reached through introspection one realizes that the interests of others do not run counter to our own interests. One can see through the tendencies that cause our routine anxieties.

The Self (Purusha) is free of any limitations. She simply observes, becomes aware of the multiple facets of the object observed, of experience felt, and perception is free of any limitation or distortion. The relationship between the observer and the observed is such that one is at peace. Such perception is described as 'pure seeing' by the Self that we are born with. Pure seeing brings knowledge of the Self.

Key words: Mind, Reality, Self

Sutras 17-22 describe the result of a mind at peace.

<u>Cognition-based absorption</u>

I.17   vitarka vicara ananda asmitarupa anugamat samprajnatah

वि तर्क विचार आनंद अस्मिता रूपा अनुगमात संप्रज्नत: ।

   vitarka: conjecture; vicara: reason; ananda: bliss;

asmitarupa: sense of Self; anugamat: with association;

samprajnatah: know accurately

Practice and detachment result in four types of Samadhi (absorption): self-analysis, synthesis, bliss, and the experience of pure being. This is samprajnata, or cognitive, Samadhi.

Samadhi is the state of being intensely absorbed in an experience, and is the process of interiorization whereby one reaches deep within the consciousness. 'Samprajnata' or cognitive Samadhi (absorption) is based on experience related to knowledge. To make sense of a thought or emotion, we begin with making a conjecture ('vitarka') regarding what it means. It means considering its different aspects. This initial query is followed by thoughtful consideration ('vichara'), which is concentrating on certain aspects of that experience, perhaps analyze and reason about it. This can provide new insights regarding it. When the irrelevant is discarded one gets a better idea about what really matters, and that can usher in a blissful state of peace ('ananda'). This inner level is the one of bliss, of the pleasure and happiness that motivate us. When at the sensual level that is the basic and simplest form and at the higher level is the contentment and satisfaction that one feels upon completing or achieving something at the end of properly performed actions. It is however, only a fragment of the real and permanent bliss of the Self. It is the bliss that one finds in serving others. At this stage other objects, thoughts and emotions, are left behind. Next, continued concentration brings about an understanding of the innate, basic Self, that is free of the limitations on perception due to ego ('asmita'), or our sense of individuality (asmitarupa).

These are the four different states of absorption. Together they share the common basis of thoughts and emotions and belong to what is referred to as 'samprajnata' or cognition-based Samadhi. It ultimately leads to right intelligence.

Key words: Attention, Practice

Cognition-free absorption

I.18   virampratyayaya abhyasapurvah samskar sesahanyah

विरामप्रत्ययाय अभ्यासपूर्व: संस्कार शेषोन्य: ।

viram: pause; pratyaya: instrument; abhyas: practice;

purvah: previous; samskar: impressions;

sesah: remnant; anyah: other

When thoughts subside, a void arises in the mind. Staying absorbed there is another form of Samadhi. However, hidden impressions are still there, in a dormant state. Those impressions can spring up creating thoughts disturbing the mind.

In cognition based absorption, or 'samprajnata' Samadhi (referred to in Sutra I.17) the mind has an object to concentrate on. It is when there is no image of the object in the mind that one can be said to have reached 'asamprajnata' Samadhi. This state is free of any attachments, wherein previous experiences do not activate any thoughts, and silent moments between thoughts stretch. Such silent moments of absorption are without any object for focus. It is a state beyond the mind since the practitioner does not remain as a separate thinking entity.

This stage is indicative of a strong practice. However, one still needs to remain vigilant. Reverting to the usual mundane thought processes can happen. One is not immune to the hold of long held impressions that can easily arise and activate thoughts in response.

Key words: Attention, Mind, Practice

<u>Transcendence</u>

I.19   bhava-pratyayo videha-prakrti layanam

भवप्रत्ययो विदेह प्रकृति लयानाम् ।

bhava: becoming; pratyayo: means; videha: bodiless, without material existence; prakriti: the world; layanam: merged, dissolved

In this state, one may feel body-less, as if merged in the subtlest elements of existence. This is withdrawal from everything.

This Sutra refers to the practitioner in a state of deep cognition-free absorption, the practitioner can transcend the awareness of bodily existence. She can stay deeply absorbed in the subtlest form of existence, and attains higher intelligence (Buddhi). Experiences are not recognized or felt anymore. Long held impressions weaken. This is also the mark of success in the long practice.

Key words: Attention, Mind, Reality

<u>Practice Essentials</u>

I.20   sraddha virya smriti samadhi prajna purvakah itaresam

श्रद्धा वीर्य स्मृति समाधि प्रज्ञा पूर्वक इतरेषाम् ।

sraddha: faith; virya: vigor; smriti: memory; samadhi: total absorption; prajna: super awareness;

purvakah: preceding; itaresam: other

For attaining a state of complete absorption, one needs faith or trust in the practice, plus will, memory, and wisdom gained through contemplation.

The various stages through which a meditating practitioner goes through are easier to access for some and may be not so for some others. It also takes will to continue practicing. For some, the states of complete absorption referred to in the earlier sutras can be easily attained through trust and faith in the efficacy of sustained practice. That faith provides the energy for maintaining a dedicated practice and thereby helps in establishing memory about the state of concentration. That feeling of concentration then becomes habitual. Remembering the calming experiences of practice provides the motivation to continue.

Wisdom is gained because of detached reflection upon experiences, and a realistic weighing of options and their consequences. It comes with self-knowledge. Introspection is about learning to be attentive in an objective way to one's emotions, desires and views that are part of any experience. Going back to the original experience, and understanding it, leads to Buddhi, the discriminative type of intelligence. The word prajna in this Sutra refers to a certain higher type of pure awareness or intellect that is free of any limitations. It appears when the mind is focused.

Sense impressions and superficial sense of identity cease to retain their hold on thoughts and actions. With that awareness one understands the nature of reality and of the 'Self' within. It is like attaining spiritual vision. The Self watches but does not react and one gains an intuitive understanding of everything and that is that inner wisdom.

Key words: Attention, Practice, Self, Wisdom

A strong Practice

1.21 tivra-samveganam asannah

तीव्र संवेगामानाम् आसन्ना: ।

tivra: intense; samvega: desire for ultimate relief;
samveganam: those who are vehement;

asannah: drawn near

The state of deep absorption (Samadhi) is reachable for those who apply themselves intensely.

Practice, in Sanskrit, is 'abhyasa'. Abhi, the prefix means intentionally moving or going towards (something). One of the meanings of the verb 'as' is 'to do anything without interruption.' The word 'abhyasa' therefore means persevering in the effort and without interruption. Some practitioners are intense and enthusiastic in pursuing their goals. They quietly persevere in their mission and have a strong resolve. They can put aside any distraction. These practitioners can achieve the deep concentration needed for advancing in the discipline.

Key words: Attention, Practice

Types of practitioners

I.22   mrdu madhya adhimatratvat tatah api visesah

मृदु मध्य अधिमात्रत्वात् तत: अपि विशेष: ।

mrdu: soft, modest; madhya: intermediate; adhimatratvat: steady, keen; tatah: thence; api: also;

visesah: differentiation

Some practitioners are not as committed, some are average, and some who are keen in their practice.

There are different types of practitioners. To succeed in any endeavor, it takes commitment. Some can be very devoted or keen, and some are in between. Therefore, depending on their dedication their progress is either slow or quick. The degree of enthusiasm and dedication of the practitioner matters in terms of how soon one can reach the objective of the state of total absorption. Too much zeal is self-defeating. Properly directed zeal, focused on self-exploration, is important. When balance and harmony between will and tenacity along the path are maintained, success is more likely to be achieved.

Key words: Practice

Sutras 23-29 are about the effectiveness of focusing on any preferred deity or principle in bringing peace.

Surrender to a higher power

I.23 Ishvarapranidhanadva

ईश्वर प्रणिधानात् वा ।

Ishwara: God; pranidhanat: devotion, meditation; va: or

Or the mind may be calmed by total surrender to and profound meditation on God.

New meditators often find it difficult to concentrate and throughout the Yoga Sutras there are other helpful options suggested. Faith, vigor, and steady practice are helpful towards staying on the path. What matters is a humble attitude while striving to attain the objective of calming the mind. For that, this Sutra says that it helps to concentrate on ones preferred representation of divinity.

The word 'Ishwar' refers to God, yet it does not limit a practitioner to a specific form of God. The focus can be in the form of one's desired figure, icon or symbol, in whatever religion one may follow. One may have faith in and devotion for any special object or concept. It can be an ideal or a person. Wherever one finds inspiration; divinity, in art, in nature, or a cause towards humanity; that becomes one's desired deity and teacher. It helps in the practice of introspection. Contemplation and meditation is turning inwards and understanding life experiences.

The word 'pranidhanat' stands for prayer, meditation or contemplation. Devotion is orientation of thought and action for attaining a certain goal. Besides providing a focus, this approach represents an attitude of surrender and humility. It is spiritually uplifting and it also softens the ego.

Key words: Attention, Practice

<u>Reverent practice</u>

I.24   klesha-karma-vipakasayair aparamrstah purusavisesah
Ishvarah

क्लेषकर्म विपाक शयैर अपरामृष्ट: पुरुषचिशेष ईश्वर: ।

klesha: affliction; karma: action; vipaka: result; asayaih:
abode; aparamrstah: untouched; purusa: being, person;
visesah: special; Ishvarah: God

Ishwar is a distinct being/Purusha, totally free of conflicts, unaffected by karma, and untouched by long-term karmic imprints.

Yoga philosophy is about Purusha and Prakriti, or roughly speaking, about beings and the changeable material world. In Yoga, God (Ishwar) is described as a special person who is untouched by the common afflictions that limit and distort our understanding of reality.

The Yoga philosophy is mostly secular and the inclusion of God in the Sutra is for accommodating the believers, yet without compromising the essential themes within its philosophical framework. Devotion and surrender of ego play an important part in the Yoga discipline and the inclusion of Ishwar or God in Patanjali's Yoga Sutras plays an important role in that. Patanjali made Ishwar part of psycho-mental techniques for quieting thoughts, and for finding freedom from grief causing afflictions, the 'klesha'. Karma is the account of one's choices in the past. This account is carried forward at the time of death to influence future lives. The effects or fruits of actions are retained in the form of deep seated dormant and potential urges that become afflictions. These afflictions in turn are strengthened through repeated actions.

Patanjali had a specific definition of Ishwar (God). He defines Ishwar as a Supreme Being who is totally free from afflictions and from fruits of action, without any bondage to the past or the future, and refers to him as 'Purush-visesa', a special Purusha. That special Purusha supports, maintains harmony, and protects the good in everyone and is understood and expressed through various forms.

BKS Iyengar said that Ishwar is Divinity in a general and a non-denominational sense. Ishwar includes various concepts of divinity. Whatever form one may feel comfortable with and closer to, it is the spirit of devotedness that matters and it allows one to put the thought of 'me, and myself' aside. It is turning inwards with a feeling of offering. Vivekananda thought that devotion to an ideal is necessary, especially for the beginner in the practice. Surrender to a higher power can reduce anxiety and fear and bring peace.

Key words: Attention, Afflictions, Mind, Practice

<u>Ishwar is all-knowing</u>

I.25   tatra niratisayam sarvadnyabijam

तत्र निरतिशयम् सर्वज्ञ बीजम् ।

tatra: in him; niratisayam: unsurpassed; sarvadnya: all-knowing; bijam: cause

God is the unexcelled seed of all knowledge.

We incrementally understand and gain knowledge. But, God represents the supreme wisdom and the ultimate level of ability to understand and know anything. Therefore, the perfect ideal for the practitioner to focus on.

Key words: Practice

Ishwar is the supreme teacher

I.26 sa esah purvesam api guruh kalen anavacchedat

स एष पूर्वेषाम् अपि गुरु: कालेन अनवच्छेदात् ।

sa: that; esah: Purusha; purvesam: foremost; api: also; guruh: master; kalena: time; anavacchedat: unlimited

Ishwar, the supreme purusha, is the first and foremost teacher, and unconditioned by time.

Ishwar is the supreme teacher who is not limited in any way; either by time, place, or circumstance. This is consistent with the concept of Ishwar as defined in Sutra I.24, as a special Purusha who is free of all afflictions. She is part of every generation throughout history and therefore ever-present. She provides guidance to all practitioners looking for support and thus is important.

Key words: Practice

'Aum' is the sacred symbol

I.27 tasya vacakah pranavah

तस्य वाचक: प्रणव: ।

tasya: her; vacakah: symbol; pranavah: the sacred syllable 'Om'.

She (God) is expressed through the sound of the sacred syllable OM, called 'pranava'.

The ancient Hindus believed that there is a cosmic intelligence that exists everywhere, and in all of us. The universe is also full of energy; the stars, the planets, the oceans and life itself are all in a constant state of motion. All these have a natural rhythm and pulse. The pulsing vibration of the universe supposedly created the first primordial sound, the unheard, unstruck sound, or the 'anahata nada'. 'Anahata' is unstruck and 'nada' is the inner sound. That unstruck and inner sound of the universe is called Om also referred to as Aum. It is a powerful sound. That sound also emanates from within the body.

Om is frequently called the pranava, literally meaning "humming." (The word pranava is derived from the word 'nava' with the prefix 'pra' which means ever fresh, ever new.) 'Om' or Aum represents Ishwar and is used for deep contemplation and by renunciates for meditation.

Key word: Practice

Repetition of 'Aum' mantra

I.28   tad japah tad artha bhavanam

तद् जप: तद् अर्थ भावनम् ।

tad: that; japah: recitation; artha: meaning; bhavana: realization

The mantra 'aum' is to be repeated constantly with feeling, realizing its full significance.

Constant repetition of the mantra 'aum', not mechanically, but with awareness about its meaning (as described in the previous Sutra) draws the mind inwards. Supposedly 'A' represents the physical, 'U' the mental, and 'M' the highly cerebral plane in the body. Another interpretation is that 'a' represents the waking state, 'u' our inner consciousness and 'm' stands for the dreamless state one is in deep sleep. This abstract yet powerful mantra is helpful in attaining the state of complete absorption, or Samadhi. It is a form of devotional offering fostering humility. Repeated recitation helps keep away distracting thoughts from the mind. Hence its importance in the Yogic endeavor.

Key words: Attention, Practice

<u>Introspection</u>

I.29   tatah pratyak chetana adhigamah api antaraya

abhavah ca

तत: प्रत्यक् चेतना अधिगम: अपि अन्तराय अभाव: च ।

tatah: then; pratyakchetana: introspective awareness; adhigamah: discover; api: also; antaraya: intervention; abhavah: absence; ca: and

Meditation on God with the repetition of 'Om' helps discover the inner self.

God is the all-knowing power. Concentrating on that power by constantly reciting 'Om' with a devotional attitude draws us inwards. Such introspection helps us understand our impulses and behaviors. And we come to the realization of the peace within and that our true Self is awareness. The physical and psychological well-being thus attained helps overcome any obstacles (described in the next Sutra) in the Yogic endeavor.

Key words: Attention, Self

Sutras 30-33 list the difficulties commonly experienced in maintaining attention and suggests different ways of overcoming those.

Obstacles to practice

I-30   vyadhi styna samsaya pramada alasya avirati
bhranti darsana alabdha bhumikatva anavasthit tatvani
chitta vikshepa te antarayah

व्याधिस्त्यान संशय प्रमाद आलस्य अविरति भ्रान्ति दर्शन अलब्ध
भूमिकत्व अनवस्थित् तत्वानि चित्त विक्षेपा: ते अंतराया: ।

vyadhi: sickness; styna: inertia; samsaya: doubt, indecision; pramada: negligence; alasya: laziness; avirati: without moderation; bhranti: false; darsana: vision; alabdha: non-attaining; bhumikatva: stage; anavasthitatvani: instability; chitta: consciousness; viksepah: distraction; te: these; antarayah: obstacles

The obstacles to continued practice are illness, inertia, doubt, heedlessness, laziness, indiscipline of the senses, erroneous views, lack of perseverance, and backsliding.

There are nine obstacles that distract and obstruct any progress in Yoga. According to BKS Iyengar some are physical, some mental, some intellectual, and some of a spiritual nature. A body affected by ailments cannot sustain the physical as well as mental energy needed for practice. Misdirected zeal is destabilizing by not delivering the expected progress. A mind that is easily distracted cannot focus its attention on the path. Doubts about the efficacy of the practice weaken the intent while unruly senses easily lead astray. When there is lack of progress, it is easy to get disheartened and become mired in self-doubt. Unless one becomes aware of such pitfalls it becomes hard to get back into practice. There can be a recurrent mental struggle as one tries to overcome the push and pull of these factors while cultivating introspective attention. One needs perseverance to overcome all such disturbances and follow the path to attain the objective in Yoga, namely, calming of thoughts.

Key words: Attention, Practice

<u>Distracted minds</u>

I.31   duhkha daurmanasya angamejayatva svasa prasvasah
vikshepa sahabhuvah

दु:ख दौर्मन्यस्य अंगमेजयत्व श्वास प्रश्वास: विक्षेप सहभुव: ।

duhkha: pain; daurmanasya: despair;

angamejayatva: unsteadiness of the body;

svasa: Inspritaion; prasvasah: expiration; vikshepa: scattered attention; sahabhuvah: concurrent

Distractions bring distress, despair, trembling of the body, and disturbed breathing. They further agitate and distress the mind.

What are the symptoms of a distracted mind? The first is pain, indicative of disharmony or imbalance. When there is some inner conflict and one is wavering between conflicting options; introspective self-examination is the option for finding relief. When that relief is not found, the pain deepens into despair which manifests as trembling in the body and uneven breathing. These are indications of the influence of some imbalance as well as a distracted mind.

It should be noted in this context that in our daily life we may not experience these specific symptoms, except feeling varying levels of stress. Nonetheless, they do affect our body/mind; eventually manifesting in the form of lower energy levels, hunched shoulders, eating disorders, irritability due to unmet desires and aspirations, depression and anxiety issues, elevated blood pressure, and other stress induced ailments. And unless and until they are addressed those effects can persist and enhance the strain experienced. Various Yoga practices provide options for distancing oneself from these experiences, and an attitude of devotion and surrender provides the strength needed for overcoming them.

Key words: Attention, Mind, Practice

Focused attention

I.32   tat-pratisedhartham eka-tattvabhysah

तत्प्रतिषेधार्थम् एकतत्व अभ्यास: ।

tat: that; pratisedhartham: for prevention; eka: single; tattva: principle; abhysah: practice

Adherence to single minded effort helps overcome obstacles to practice.

The mind tends to run in different directions. It is drawn towards the outer world of experiences. Without the strength of dedication, overcoming such distractions becomes difficult. Keeping attention focused is needed and helpful to weaken any distracting tendencies. The mind becomes quiet when the various distractions are weakened. While focusing on God or recitation of mantras such as "Om' is helpful, there are other options too. It helps to be selective in the choice of focus. Things and interests suited for individual temperament, passionate interests, are especially helpful for keeping the attention engaged. Then, there is a greater likelihood of overcoming problems, listed in Sutra I.30, due to a distracted mind. That can help sustain attention.

Key words: Attention, Practice

<u>Positive attitudes</u>

I.33   maitri karuna mudita upeksanam sukha duhkha punya apunya visayanam bhavanahtah cittaprasadanam

मैत्री करुणा मुदिता उपेक्षाणाम् सुख दु:ख पुण्य अपुण्य विषयाणाम् भावनात: चित्त प्रसादनम् ।

maitri: friendliness; karuna: compassion; mudita: delight; upeksanam: indifference; sukha: happiness; duhkha: sorrow; punya: virtue; apunya: vice; visayanam: objects; bhavanahtah: feeling; citta: mind; prasadanam: favorable disposition

Through cultivation of friendliness, compassion, joy, and indifference to pleasure and pain, to virtue and vice, consciousness becomes favorably disposed, serene and benevolent.

In our reactions to those around us, maintaining a certain balance is needed, and it is beneficial for maintaining peace within and with another. For that Patanjali recommends cultivating certain attitudes of a benevolent nature, attitudes that are based on distancing oneself from self-occupation, small-mindedness and rigidity. These include cultivation of friendliness, feeling compassion for someone suffering, sharing the joys of others instead of feeling jealous about their achievements, not making too much of one's own pleasures, pains, and virtues, and being more tolerant of faults and vices of others. These various attitude practices are about increasing the understanding of and developing sensitivity not only to one's own mind and body, but also to those of others.

To achieve that, it helps to reorient the mind and not only separate from the undesirable but also actively pursue the desired states of mind. The mind cannot hold opposite thoughts at the same time. Holding on to the positive comes with sustained effort. Paying attention to and adhering to such discipline is mind changing. Any type of transformation comes from attention. That attention needs to be free of compulsive egotistic needs, of doubts about one's ability and free of the pull of ambitions.

Not following such attitudes and instead vying to get where others are, or ignoring the plight of the less fortunate and condemning the wrong doer without understanding the wrong or the doer, is unsettling and stressful. By cultivating positive thoughts one can replace troubling ones. It is an approach based on reasoning and working with the mind. It involves changing one's overall outlook. It is purifying and it restructures the mind and behavior skillfully. This enables one to override the hold of negative conditioning of the mind as we live and interact with others.

Key words: Attention, Practice, Reality

In Sutras 34-39 Patanjali states the importance of practicing meditation while maintaining a detached attitude.

<u>Breathing</u>

I.34   pracchardana vidharanabhyam va pranasya

प्रच्छर्दन विधारणाभ्याम् वा प्राणस्य ।

pracchardana: exhalation; vidharanabhyam: retention; va: or; pranasya: of breath/life force

Peace of mind is also brought about by soft and steady exhalation with passive retention after exhalation.

Breathing helps circulate life energy throughout the body; to the organs, muscles, and the brain. Breathing and mind are connected. Normally our breathing occurs automatically and we are not aware of the sub-processes involving inhalation, exhalation and the short pauses in between. The mind settles in a peaceful and serene state when attention is focused on breathing; softly and slowly, and retaining the pauses in between, comfortably. As the body stays still, the mind is drawn away from existential thoughts, about oneself or about a life experience. The pauses separate and hold those quiet moments still. These usher in physiological and psychological effects that are helpful in calming the mind.

Key words: Attention, Mind, Practice

<u>Concentration on senses</u>

I.35   visayavati va pravrttih utpanna manasah sthiti nibandhani

विषयवति वा प्रवृत्ति: उत्पन्न मनस: स्थिति निबन्धनि ।

visayavati: related to an object; va: or; pravrttih: pursuit; utpanna: acquired; manasah: mind; sthiti: state;

nibandhani: helpful

The mind focused on senses elevates perceptions.

The mind is steadied when one concentrates on emerging sensations. Such attention directed at an object helps gain a clear perception thereof. By attending to developing sensations we perceive the subtleties associated with any experience. Such heightened sensory awareness, and direct perception are without any coloring, and without ushering a tendency to react. Otherwise, that coloring and conditioning prevents real understanding of the experience. And we miss out on its essence.

Some say that concentrating on hearing subtle sounds, smells and tastes are also effective ways of attaining a deep meditative state. Shutting off the obvious and directing the attention, instead, towards the hidden also makes one aware of until then unrecognized sensations.

Key words: Attention, Mind, Practice

<u>Positive thoughts</u>

I.36   visoka va jyotismati

विशोका वा ज्योतिष्मती ।

visoka: serene; va: or; jyotismati: luminous

Concentration needs a mind free of worries and in a tranquil state.

In this Sutra Patanjali reiterates that being selective about which emotions to attend to is an important step. There are many ways for doing that. Positive feelings are not hard to identify. Simply recognizing that one is alive and breathing; feeling the warmth of sunshine that sustains everything, and opening the heart to these blessings connects us to the warmth and contentment within. A form of insight arises without a thought process attached to it; there is no choice-making involved, and it is impersonal in nature. The repose felt in this state takes the mind off other things, and one discovers different dimensions of the object of focus.

As we face life's challenges, it helps to reach out for the light of happiness within us. When one concentrates on that state, which is free of conflict and grief, and has the quality of luminance; the mind becomes steady. The conflict and grief free quality comes with letting go of the hold of 'rajas', or active energy, and 'tamas', or inertia, two of the three 'Gunas'. The illumination referred to is knowledge that represents understanding of subtle things, the glow of happiness felt when experiencing something wholesome. Severing the link of thought to unhappy, sorrowful events and experiences is freeing and it opens the mind for receiving calming and happy thoughts. Remembering and reliving feelings such as compassion, gratitude and joy nurture calm and peaceful states of mind. Contentment is an important part of self-discipline.

Desires hold us captive, making us more self-centered. For weakening their hold on us, we need to shift attention to other beings and their needs. When we concentrate on the breath there is no desire involved. When one lets likes and dislikes go, the illusion of a separate self, separate and apart from others, also goes. There is freedom from wanting. That freedom one nurtures through high ideals such as 'ahimsa' or non-harming and truthfulness, and by containing greedy tendencies. Keeping the attention focused then becomes easier.

Key words: Attention, Ethics, Mind, Reality

<u>Think of the sages</u>

I.37 vita-raga-visayam va cittam

वीतराग विषयम् वा चित्तम् ।

> vita: free from; raga: desire; visayam: object; va: or; cittam: the mind

Or, the mind becomes steady by contemplating on enlightened sages who are free of desires, and are calm and tranquil.

This Sutra provides another practical way for attaining peace. It says that peace can be attained by making the mind free of attachments, or by meditating about those who have demonstrated freedom from desires. Thinking about sages and spiritual figures is inspiring and helpful in resisting the pull of desires. Various sages exemplify qualities such as strong will, altruism, egoless-ness, faith, to name a few, and these can help draw us out of ourselves and thus help the mind.

One can also learn and emulate leaders and spiritual guides who have demonstrated freedom from mundane desires. Connections with spiritual guides and groups provide real and therefore more tangible meditative focus than some abstract ideas or objects. The idea is to seek inspiration from others who have been known to have found peace. They help further one's own ability to withstand the pull of desires and realize one's own potential.

Looking up to something and to someone also means rising above the rigid hold of ego. The more one practices such release from self-centered thinking, the easier it becomes. One becomes more open to new thoughts and new ways of being. Finding the appropriate ideals is not always easy and needs vigilance. Superficial impressions can mislead.

Key words: Attention, Afflictions, Practice

<u>Meditate on dreams or on sleep</u>

I.38   svapna nidra jnana alambanam va

स्वप्र निद्रा ज्ञान आलंबनम् वा ।

svapna: dream; nidra: dreamless sleep; jnana: knowledge; alambanam: depends on; va: also

(The mind can become steady) by focusing attention on insights gained in dreams and deep dreamless sleep.

In the deep sleep state, there are no ongoing thoughts and one feels at peace. In the dream state consciousness is dissociated from the body although still connected to the world of experiences. The images and sensations received in dreams can provide significant information and insights. According to Jung, dreams can give us the guidance we need in finding a way out of the problems of both inner and outer life. Neuroscientist Rudolfo Llianas and Sigmund Freud allude to the quality of dreaming in which there is a shift away from any sense of a tightly demarcated self. It is as if we are looking at the action in our dreams as both the observer and the observed. By examining our dreams, we can discover things about ourselves, and about reality.[1]

Keeping the mind on dreams is a useful channel for attention regulation. Meditating on pleasant, wholesome and spiritual dreams is advisable. The objective is to attain the total peace that we associate with deep sleep. The Vedic interpretation is that when the mind is in deep sleep it is in contact with its source, the Self, God or Brahman.

Key words: Attention, Practice

1. Siegel Daniel J., 2018. Aware: The Science and Practice of Presence. Tarcherperigee, New York.

Choices for meditation

I.39   yatha abhimata dhyanat va

यथा अभिमत ध्यानात् वा ।

yatha: as; abhimata: preferred; dhyana: meditation; va: or

By meditating on any object of one's choice, one attains steadiness of mind.

Meditation is not a very easy practice for any novice. Given the different temperaments of new meditators, it is helpful to choose a meditation practice that is compatible with individual preferences and inclinations. Among the various practices referred to in these previous Sutras are, for example: concentrating on breathing, on a deity or personage of one's choice, uplifting dreams, peaceful and serenity enhancing experiences, or reciting a mantra. By meditating on an object of one's choice it is easier to attain steadiness of mind and the blissful feeling that comes with it. This does not mean that one should concentrate on getting some object like a car. Because that is more likely to usher in a feeling of deprivation instead of peace.

BKS Iyengar postulated that asana practice done in a meditative manner, is an option available for modern practitioners. Concentrating on any disciplined experience makes us more receptive to it and keeps the mind on the moment. The past and present become open whereas the future recedes from awareness. When anxieties are weakened, understanding of our multifaceted reality is enhanced. By choosing a practice one does not like or feel comfortable with, results in resistance to continue and that becomes counter-productive.

Key words: Practice

The transformative effects of practice are listed thereafter in Sutras 40-45.

<u>Understanding of small and large</u>

I.40   param anu parama mahattva antah asya vasikarah

परमाणु परम महत्वान्तोस्य वशिकार: ।

param smallest; anu: particle; parama: ultimate; mahattva: infinity; antah: extending up to; asya: of this; vasikarah: mastery

Mastery of contemplation gives power over smallest as well as the largest object.

An accomplished meditator gains mastery over mind. Ability to understand oneself is understanding multiple aspects of reality. Whether the object of contemplation is minute or large, for an accomplished practitioner, it does not present any problem in sustaining focused attention on it. Such attention results in understanding of and attaining mastery over these objects.

Key words: Attention, Practice, Reality

Samapatti: The state of total absorption

I.41 ksina-vrtteh abhijatasya iva maneh grahitir grahana
grahyesu tatstha tad-ajnanata samapattih

क्षीणवृत्ते अभिजातस्य इवमणे ग्रहितिर ग्रहण ग्राह्येषु तटस्थ तद
अज्ञानता समापत्ति: ।

ksina: weak; vrtteh: modifications of mind; abhijatasya:
inborn; iva: like; maneh: flawless jewel; grahitir: knower;
grahana: knowing; grahyesu: cognized object; tatstha:
stable; tad: its, ajnanata: taking of the color; samapattih:
balanced state

In the case of one whose thoughts have been completely sub-
dued, the cognizer, cognition and cognized are absorbed in one
another. The knowing mind becomes like a transparent jewel
resting on a colored surface, purely reflecting everything. This
quality of sensitive reflection is called yoga, integration. It is
achieving transformation of the afflicted consciousness.

Reality consists of the observer, the observing instrument,
and the observed object. In linking the observed to the observer,
the quality of the observing instrument matters. If the instrument
is flawed it means that the observer receives either a tainted or
incomplete knowledge of the observed object. Full knowledge
depends on the observer's ability to perceive different aspects of
an object. But the ability to perceive both the gross and the subtle
aspects of any object or experience is there, only when the observing instrument, the body/mind, is clear of any limitations.

When natural tendencies and inherent limitations are becalmed and the mind is totally focused, we arrive at the direct and
unchanged understanding of what we see and experience.

Cleared of the hold of our conditioned perceptions, everything that we can see and know appears as it is and not how we expect it to be. The yoga discipline is about how to achieve this transformation in how we see and experience the world. When the mind is so transformed, it is in a balanced state. Perception of the seen object, or the felt experience is transmitted through the body clearly and directly to the Self, the awareness within. Then there is no separation of the Self from the seen or from the instrument of seeing, that is the body/mind.

A completely still mind in this state is like a pure transparent jewel. It reflects the pure awareness within us that is unconditioned and unaffected. The practitioner reaches the stage at which one can take in the totality of experience, with the understanding of the multiple facets thereof. There is no interpretation or meaning assigned to reality and reality is perceived as it is. All the misconceptions, impurities that cloud the mind are removed. Things are observed at the most basic level moment by moment. This state of mental absorption, described as 'samapatti', is often compared to a crystal that is totally devoid of any impurity. The mind has a vision of the world that is so clear that like that crystal it reflects exactly whatever is put next to it. It does not modify anything, subtle or gross, minute or large, and everything becomes clear and totally perceptible.

Key words: Practice, Self, Reality

Cognition based transformation

I.42   tatra sabda artha jnana vikalpaih sankirna savitarka samapattih

तत्र शब्द अर्थ ज्ञान विकल्पै: संकीर्ण स वि तर्क समापत्ति: ।

> tatra: there; sabda: word; artha: real meaning; jnana: knowledge; vikalpaih: imagination; sankirna: intermingled; savitarka: thoughtful; samapattih: transformation

In contemplative meditation when the word, knowledge and real meaning are blended and become special knowledge, the mind shifts from one to the other.

How do we go about knowing reality? This Sutra describes the initial impression when we see or experience something. The initial perception is coarse and, therefore, of a lower quality. The mind considers the word describing it, and the sense experience thereof. Usually, the information that these provide tends to be imprecise and incomplete. For example, when one concentrates on an object like a rose, for someone who does not know what a rose is, the word does not mean anything. For one who is familiar with it, it suggests a certain flower. But the name rose can be attached to any other object and any sensations can be ascribed to any experience. It is a form of conceptualizing.

Impressions, whether word based, description based, or meaning based; separate and overlap. Attention shifts from one impression to the other. Thoughts arise and they usually tend to be clouded by memories or by some feeling attached to those.

On the other hand, when the mind is focused, all these levels of cognition, the word, object, experience, and our feelings and knowledge thereof, arise together. And one arrives at the intuitive understanding of the essence of any object or experience. This is higher quality perception.

Key words: Mind, Reality

<u>Cognition-free transformation</u>

I.43   smriti parisuddhau svarupa sunya iva artha matra nirbhasa
nirvitarka

स्मृति परिशुध्दौ स्वरुप शून्य इव अर्थ मात्र नि र्भास निर्वितर्क ।

smriti: memory; parisuddhi: purification; sva: own; rupa:
form; sunya: without; iva: as it were; artha: object; matra:
only; nirbhasa: shining forth; nirvitarka: above thought

In 'nirvitarka samapatti' or ultra-cognitive absorption, memory is
cleansed and real knowledge shines through the mind.

This Sutra refers to the state of thought-free absorption
without the support of any form or label for the object of meditative focus. When absorbed in a meditative state, when one distances the mind from any memories and impressions that the
mind holds, subjectivity is removed and there is no held-over
conceptualization. Objects are not seen through the lens of past
impressions. Instead they are seen, as they really are at that
moment. When concepts are free of tangible truths, what remains
is pure perceptual truth. This absorptive state is, therefore, free of
the hold of inferred knowledge. One then perceives things as they
really are and there is no interference of words, their meaning
and the knowledge they provide, in the way of pure seeing. Pure
seeing is perception that is fresh, free of any previous impressions and not hindered or limited by any afflictions, and experiences. The old mind is thus transformed into the new enlightened
instrument of perception.

Key words: Attention, Mind, Practice, Reality

Absorption, with and without reflection

I.44   etaiva savicara nirvicara ca suksma visaya vyakhyata

एतयैव सविचार निर्विचार च सूक्ष्म विषय व्याख्याता ।

> etaiva: by this; savicara: Samadhi with reflection; nirvicara: Samadhi without reflection; ca: and; suksmavisaya: involving subtle objects; vyakhyata: explained

Absorption, with or without reflection, explains subtle objects.

After the initial introspective practice of examining one's perceptions regarding the gross form of an object, attention is focused on something subtle such as a thought, the emotion it represents and analysis and reasoning behind it. This is 'vichara', the thought based understanding. The word 'vicara' is derived from vi +car, meaning progressive movement. And in this form of absorption (Samadhi) it refers to the movement of the mind away from the initial gross form to subtle levels of perception. By examining the subtle aspects of an experience by unraveling the complexities therein one can understand how the mind is conditioned. The conditioning is in the form of the hold of ego, of biases, memories and senses involved, and our tendencies favoring some of these. The objective of this practice of meditation is to break down the experience to its simplest states. This deeply analytical and introspective examination is referred to as contemplation based on thought or 'Sa-vichara Samadhi' or Samadhi with reflection.

When the deeply absorbed state moves beyond such support it is referred to as thought-free contemplation, or 'Nir-vichara Samadhi', or Samadhi without reflection. It is freedom from memory and its support. One transcends awareness of thoughts and sensations. When all the subjectivity in perception is gone, there is undisturbed calm. It is a totally transformative experience that leads to 'rtambhara prajna' or unfailing intellect. It yields self-knowledge that cannot be attained through intellectual reasoning. 'Prajna' is intelligence that leads to wisdom about the subtlest forms of objective and subjective elements of all reality.

Key words: Practice, Reality

<u>Subtle forms of objects and mental experiences</u>

I.45   suksma visayatvam ca alinga paryavasanam

सूक्ष्म विषयत्वम् च अलिङ्ग पर्यवसानम् ।

suksma: subtle; visayatva: object; ca: and; alinga: unmanifested form; paryavasanam: ending

Consciousness is the subtlest level of nature, Prakriti. When it loses its afflicted nature, and becomes pure, it has reached the subtlest level.

Nature or reality in Yoga represents all things in their observable and not so easily observable, and subtle forms. The five basic elements in all objects consist of earth, water, air, space, and energy. Anything material can be understood in terms of the balances among these elements. For example, wood has the earth element in the form of minerals, water in the sap, air circulating through its body, space in the form of pores, and the energy in the form of the various ongoing processes of assimilation and discarding of products within it. While earth and water elements are observable, air, space and energy are the subtle elements. All these emanate out of nature's subtlest form, which is the cosmic intelligence, Mahat.

The individual counter-part of cosmic intelligence is the pure intelligence within us. It is also the purest form of nature, wherein all our mental energies are in balance. Pure intelligence gets transformed through the course of life into our ordinary intelligence, our sense of 'I', and the sensory mind. Our sensory mind evolves out of our intellect and the I-ness within us. Meditation, as described in the previous Sutras, is penetrating through these layers of awareness within us until we arrive at pure intelligence. The Self within us then is closest to that subtle form of Nature, the pure intelligence.

Key words: Mind, Reality

The last five Sutras, 47-51 are about supported and support-free forms of meditative absorption.

Seed based Samadhi

I.46   ta eva sabijah samadhih

ता एव सबीज: समाधि: ।

ta: they, eva: only; sabijah: with seed; samadhih: total absorption

The states of Samadhi described in the previous sutras are dependent upon a support or seed, and are described as 'sabija'.

When objects within the realm of Prakriti, e.g., an object, a word, mantra, or a thought, provide support for meditative concentration they are called seeds for contemplation. Therefore, Samadhi (total absorption) attained using those is called Sabija Samadhi, or Samadhi with seed. These help in discovering their respective reality and for the mind to distance itself from the afflictions that shape and limit our perceptions regarding those. The two types of this Samadhi mentioned in the previous Sutras are 'Sa-vitarka' or cognition centered, and 'Sa-vicara' or reflection centered.

In these initial stages of Samadhi, 'sa-vitarka', 'sa-vicara', one descends from the superficial to deeper levels of discriminative thought. Uninterrupted meditation, while initially concentrating on an external object, helps in fully calming the fluctuating states of mind.

When no such support is used, and attention is focused on our innate awareness, it is called seedless, or 'Nirbija Samadhi'. Corresponding to the two Samadhis referred to above, Samadhi without the basis of a word and of thought is called 'Nir-vitarka', or non-conceptual, and 'Nir-vicara' or without reflection Samadhi. In these Samadhi states the mind is free of all the afflicted thoughts. It is totally becalmed and the thought of 'I' as the doer is replaced by 'I' as the 'Self'. Gradually through these states one gains total understanding of the external as well as internal realities of our experiences.

Key words: Practice, Mind

<u>Reflection-free absorption</u>

I.47 nirvicara vaisaradye adhyatma prasadah

निर्विचार वैशारद्ये अध्यात्म प्रसाद: ।

nirvicara: non-reasoning; vaisaradye: skillfulness;

adhyatma: related to soul; prasadah: clarity

From proficiency in reasoning-free absorption emerges the spiritual light.

Reason-free Samadhi is absorption that is achieved without any support. Ordinary intelligence, perception based on inference and deduction, all limit our vision; they yield partial truths and cause many of our common illusions. There is no knowledge gained about the real nature of life, or about the common threads within its diverse aspects. In the deeper stages of concentration where there is no reasoning, a refined and higher form of intelligence, wisdom, emerges. Our ordinary consciousness is cleared of all limitations and reflects things as they are.

In the state of Samadhi described above, one transcends awareness of even a subtle object of concentration. It brings an undisturbed calm and is a totally transformative experience. It yields self-knowledge, which cannot be gained through ordinary intellect. 'Prajna' is that higher type of intelligence that leads to wisdom about the objective and subjective elements of the material reality. Piet Mondrien, the Dutch painter said: Unconditioned by subjective feeling and ideas, behind changing natural forms, there lies changeless pure reality. And Socrates said: Know thyself and know the universe.

Key words: Practice, Reality, Wisdom

<u>Truth-bearing wisdom</u>

I.48   rtam bhara tatra prajna

ऋतंभरा तत्र प्रज्ञा ।

rtam: truth; bhara: bearing; tatra: therein; prajna: insight

Consciousness dwells in wisdom and perception is direct and truth revealing.

A mental state consists of the entire field of consciousness with the objective universe reflected in it. As our mental fields expand and succeed one another, each has its center of interest, around which the objects of which we are less attentively conscious fade at the margins. These margins are so faint that their limits are unassignable. Some mental fields are narrow and some are wide. Usually when we experience a wide field we rejoice. We then see the whole truth together, and often get glimpses of inter-relations at the margins. At other times, times of drowsiness, illness, or fatigue, our fields may narrow almost to a point and we find ourselves correspondingly oppressed and contracted.

The meditative discipline opens the vast field of a mental state. It brings the realization that the universe is the manifestation of reality revealed in its expansive entirety. It holds the true essence of all things and there is a material and moral order in it. This wisdom is a refined form of intelligence. As a result, perceptions are direct, clear and true.

Key words: Mind, Wisdom

Total understanding

I. 49 sruta anumana prajnabhyam anyavisaya visesa arthatvat

श्रुत अनुमान प्रज्ञाभ्याम् अन्य विषय विशेष अर्थत्वात् ।

sruta: heard; anumana: inference; prajnabhyam: from the wisdom of insight; anya: other; visaya: object; visesa: special property; arthatvat: purpose

This truth bearing knowledge and wisdom is distinct from and beyond the knowledge gleaned from books, testimony or inference.

An earlier Sutra (I.7) mentioned that we get knowledge by direct cognition, through inference, or as a testimony from a reliable source. Sometimes knowledge that the senses deliver is supplemented with some other relevant bits of information or testimony from other reliable sources. The senses help cognizing objects, but errors can occur in that. Inference and testimony too are subject to errors. In all these the intellect plays a role. But the intellect generally cannot grasp the whole reality associated with an object.

In the deep object-free meditative state that results in total absorption (Samadhi), perceptions are transformed. One gains an intrinsic knowledge and understanding of reality. Our intuitive consciousness perceives the object/experience in the context of the whole. Such perception is free of errors, distortions and un-marred by previous impressions. For example, we can sense the approximate position and relative size of things that we may normally be unaware of, as in darkness. But the same setting, properly lighted, provides a much better picture thereof. Similarly, intuitive understanding is truth bearing knowledge, knowledge that is complete, and it encompasses gross and, as well as, subtle aspects of any object/experience.

Rtam is the cosmic order that is the eternal and inviolable material, moral and spiritual order. In the above mentioned higher state of consciousness, called prajna, such order within its wide setting, is revealed. One perceives the right and true manifestation of everything. It is direct and unfiltered. It is the insightful, mature wisdom.

Key words: Mind, Practice, Wisdom

Deactivated conditioning

I.50 tajjah samskarah anya samskara pratibandhi

तज्ज संस्कार: अन्य संस्कार प्रतिबन्धी ।

tajjah: born of; samskarah: subliminal impressions; anyasamskara: other impressions; pratibandhi: contradicting

A new life begins with this truth bearing light. The previous impressions are left behind.

Upon attaining the wisdom that the deep meditative experience delivers, simple observation becomes free of conditioning, preconceptions and habitual perception patterns. The Indian sage Ramana Maharishi[1] said: Hearing the truth is the first state, 'sravana'. If the understanding is not firm, one must practice 'manana', reflection, and uninterrupted contemplation on it, 'nididhyasa'. These two processes scorch the seeds of 'samskaras' so that they are rendered ineffective.

There is a sense of relief when the 'samskaras', the subliminal impressions that affect our perceptions, are suspended. As the practice continues one becomes aware of one's own habitual patterns and we become free of them. There are sensations in the body that are activated when we observe something with our pre-conditioned mind. Because of such conditioning the body can become dull and desensitized by set in patterns of feelings and they lead to the same type of reactive and restricted thinking. Such sensations disappear with the subliminal impressions. There is clarity of vision and that is a peaceful state.

What happens when old impressions are left behind and new ones do not arise? Stripped of any conditioning influences, these are less likely to have a distracting influence that affect actions in response, immediately, or in the future. Under those conditions, one is more likely to act for the benefit of others. This is the concept of 'nishkama karma', desire-free actions that do not bind us in any way.

Key words: Mind, Practice, Wisdom

1. Ramana Maharishi, 1985. Be as You Are: The Teachings of Sri Ramana Maharshi. Edited by David Godman, Penguin Books.

Seedless Samadhi and a free mind

I. 51 tasya api nirodhe sarva-nirodhat nirbijah samadhih

तस्यापि निरोधे सर्व निरोध निर्बीजि: समाधि: ।

tasya: of this; api: too; nirodhe: restraining; sarva: all; nirodhat: checking; nirbijah: seedless; samadhih: total absorption

Seedless Samadhi is when the mind is free of all subtle impressions, and there are no new ones arising.

When one is in a state of total absorption, without support of any object or thought for concentration, the mind is settled in peace. This peace stays in the mind and with continued practice such moments persist. The practice of staying detached helps achieve a state of experiencing the pure Self, free of the sense of individuality as commonly perceived, free of intellectual, and sense perceptions. When the imprints of experiences on the conscious, sub-conscious, unconscious and super conscious mind disappear all illusions disappear. The mind is clear and open.

Key word: Mind

———————

Chapter 4

II.   Practice (Sadhana)

In this chapter, Patanjali addresses beginning practitioners in the spiritual practice of Yoga. It deals with the body, senses and the mind. The art of practice, introspection and meditative absorption, are the important subject areas.

The following two Sutras introduce the beginner to the method of action in spiritual practice.

<u>What is Kriya Yoga?</u>

II.1   tapah svadhyaya Ishwarpranidhanani kriyayogah

तप: स्वाध्याय ईश्वर प्रणिधानानि क्रिया योग:।

tapah: austerity; svadhyaya: self-study and self-knowledge through scriptures; Ishwar: God; pranidhanani: surrender; kriya: action;

The three steps in the yoga of action are; burning zeal in practice, self-understanding, and total devotion to God.

This Sutra introduces the three important components of the Yoga of practice. Kriya is action and that action includes three practices; 'tapas', 'svadhyaya', and 'Ishwar pranidhana'. 'Tapas' is the energy invested in an undertaking. It is described as austerity or sturdy self-discipline – mental, moral, and physical. No venture is successful without some degree of self-discipline and humility. It entails an initial curiosity that is backed by intellectual understanding of the undertaking and is supported by the ability to sustain through a disciplined activity. Momentary pleasure can distract and difficulties can seem unsurmountable. Setting up boundaries helps sustain strong commitment, and continued initial enthusiasm.

'Svadhyaya' is study of oneself, and of sacred literature, which provide direction in the venture. Self-study means thinking about oneself in the sense of getting to know one's own character, one's strengths and one's weaknesses; learning to know one's failings. For self-examination, introspection and study of sacred literature are helpful. Willingness to learn from others matters and is important. We are emotionally attached to the familiar and loosening that attachment depends on how sustained the effort is to overcome it.

'Ishwar pranidhana' is complete surrender to God. Devotion nurtures humility. This eases the hold of ego that can lead to either over-zealous leaps, or doubts that hold one back. It also can moderate euphoria on success or dejection when there is failure. The three conditions listed in this Sutra, e.g., conviction, self-understanding, and devotion; present three basic and necessary supports for success in any undertaking.

Key words: Mind, Practice

<u>What does it achieve?</u>

II.2   samadhi bhavanarthah klesa tanukaranarthasca

समाधि भावनार्थः क्लेश तनूकरणार्थश्च ।

samadhi: total absorption; bhavanarthah: for bringing about; klesa: affliction; tanukaranarthasca: for reducing

The practice of Yoga reduces afflictions and leads to Samadhi.

Our thoughts and actions stand in the way of attaining the peaceful and illuminating state of total absorption. The Yoga of action described in the previous Sutra helps weaken the limitations due to these. We immerse ourselves in various activities, yet, that immersion is partial and not total. We pick and choose and that means isolating parts of the total. Those parts and fragments become the whole in our perspective when in fact they are part of a larger whole. The result is we miss the essence and that results in causing tension, confusion and misery. These become the obstacles in the path towards attaining tranquil states of mind.

The three-pronged approach to practice, dedication, self-study, and devotion, is helpful in easing tension and confusion and as a result, one can attain complete absorption in the experience of life. When the mind is free of the pull of distractions, the attention is total and insightful. Introspection helps in understanding afflictions, thereby helping overcome their hold on our thoughts and actions. And humility weakens the domination of ego.

Key words: Afflictions, Practice

Sutras 3-9 focus on the various afflictions that affect our perceptions and ultimately cause suffering.

What is 'Klesha'?

II.3   avidya asmita raga dvesha abhiniveshah kleshah

अविद्या अस्मिता राग द्वेष अभिनिवेश: क्लेशा: ।

> avidya: illusion; asmita; egoism; raga: desire, attraction; dvesha: repulsion, dislike; abhiniveshah: fear of death, of change; klesha: affliction

The five causes of afflictions that create imbalance in life are: ignorance, egoism, attachments, aversions, and insecurity or fear of changes.

Earlier in Sutra I.5 Patanjali referred to thoughts and emotions that limit our understanding and negatively affect our actions. Such thoughts and emotions are described as afflicted, or 'klishta' .'Klesha' is pain, discomfort and in Yoga philosophy it also means the causes that result in pain and discomfort. The afflictions are impurities in the mind. The mind also holds on to traces of past karma and experiences ('samskara' or 'vasanas') and those in turn can limit and negatively affect our choices. BKS Iyengar said: With asana practice one develops a greater understanding of how certain parts of our own bodies respond... This phenomenon is awakening intelligence in the body. It is an understanding that comes from experiencing it.[1] Afflictions can be caused by imbalance in the elements in the body, or can be hereditary or self-inflicted. All limitations and impurities are removed by the practice of yoga.

The concept of afflictions or 'Klesha' provides the foundation on which Yoga practices have been built. This Sutra identifies five such afflictions that are impediments to finding ease and happiness in life. These include our lack of understanding of the totality that is life ('avidya'), the self-importance and interpretation of reality that we adhere to ('asmita'), the likes ('raga') and dislikes ('dvesha') that condition our choices, and our fear of changes ('abhinivesha'). Together they prevent us from self-understanding and result in our limited and wrong cognition of reality. The following Sutras elaborate these five causes.

Key words: Afflictions, Reality

1. Iyengar, B.K.S., 2004. Light on Yoga. Harper Collins Pub. New Delhi

Afflicted states

II.4   avidya kshetram uttaresham prasupta tanu vicchinna udaranam

अविद्या क्षेत्रम् उत्तरेषाम् प्रसुप्त तनु विच्छिन्न उदराणाम् ।

avidya: lack of understanding of reality; kshetram: field; uttaresham: subsequent; prasupta: dormant; tanu: thinned; vicchinna: cut off; udaranam: fully operative

Lack of understanding of the true nature of life and of the world is the cause of all active, dormant, intermittent, or hidden, pain and sorrows.

Among the five afflictions, 'avidya', ignorance and distorted understanding of reality is the root cause of the remaining four. These four afflictions ('kleshas') include the ego, attachments and aversions, and clinging to the status quo. All the five 'kleshas', operate and make their influence felt at some time or other. Ordinarily, they are all fully operative, with varying amounts of intensity. Some may lie dormant until the appropriate conditions for their emergence appear. Or they may exist in a weakened form, waiting for a stimulus or they may at times be dominated by some other condition.

Ignorance here does not mean just lack of knowledge, but is a state of mind, how the real is perceived, taking a false view of things. Because of ignorance we take the impermanent to be permanent, or sorrow to be happiness, and the non-self for the Self. We seek knowledge to understand reality, but that is ego dominating 'avidya'. When ego asserts its strength, there is suffering and sorrow in life. The other above-mentioned 'kleshas' also owe their origin to 'avidya', ignorance. Their manifestation is of four different kinds. The first is the dormant or latent ('prasupta') state, meaning they have the potential of becoming awakened. These, for example, may stay dormant at a young age but become activated at maturity, or due to a certain situation or experience conducive to their manifestation. Sometimes they may remain inactive for two or three life cycles. When activated, they assert their influence on the mind.

The second is a weakened ('tanu') 'klesha'. By cultivating opposite feelings, such a 'klesha' can be prevented from awakening to full potency. Thus, right knowledge weakens ignorance, a weak attachment/aversion can be countered by cultivating detachment, a weak ego through self-examination, and understanding the ever-evolving nature of things averts a strong 'abhinivesha' or fear of change.

The third is the interrupted ('vicchinna') state, shifting from one state to another. An attachment for something may waver between attachment and aversion, never both at the same time.

The fourth is a fully activated ('udaranam') 'klesha'. Its presence is revealed in ongoing stress and suffering. The objective in Yoga is to overcome all such states through insight and wisdom. This is achieved by following the Yoga discipline and as the mind is becalmed.

Key words: Afflictions, Practice

Avidya defined

II.5   anitya asuci-dukhah anatmasu nitya-suci-sukha atma-khyatir avidya

अनित्य असुचि दु:ख अनात्मसु नित्य सुचि सुख आत्म ख्याति: अविद्या ।

anitya: impermanent; asuci: impure; dukhah: sorrow; anatmasu: non-Self; nitya: constant; suci: pure; sukha: joy, happiness; atma: soul; khyatih: view; avidya: ignorance

Mistaking the transient for the permanent, the impure for the pure, pain for pleasure, and confusing the superficial and material, for the real Self; all this is called lack of spiritual knowledge, or 'avidya'.

'Avidya' is ignorance that clouds our understanding of the nature of the Self, which is the awareness within us. It means ignorance about the nature of reality and constitutes a major obstacle to happiness in life. It is misperceiving reality. One thinks that one gets to know reality through personal knowledge and that the more one gets that knowledge the more one will understand the nature of reality. However, everything, our understanding, our values, the world around us, changes and evolves.

We attribute selfhood to material possessions and appearances. When our perceptions are colored by our changing viewpoints and motives; and the mind is conditioned by past built-in tendencies, likes and dislikes, our understanding is like an illusion. We think of reality as something unchanging when in fact, nothing lasts. Then we mistake ordinary pleasure for what it ultimately, and really is, which is pain. Pleasures strengthen our desires that demand satisfaction, which sets us up for disappointment sooner or later. So, the Sutra says, 'avidya' is the mistaking the transient for the permanent, the impure for the pure, pleasure for pain, and that, which is not the self for the Self. Our sense of Self, the mind, our accomplishments, what we consider to be our identity, all keep on evolving. John Updike said: Each day we wake up slightly altered, and the person we were yesterday is dead.

We are prone to make errors in comprehending the character, origin and effects of any perception or experience. From ignorance comes ego, attachments, our likes and dislikes, and our fears of changes. Ego, our likes, dislikes and fears, our ideas about self-worth, cause us to look at the world from a narrow viewpoint. They filter our perceptions, and give us a fragmented picture of reality. And when the fragments become the focus, and the whole is ignored, the result is suffering.

The stronger the hold of thoughts, and thus of 'avidya', the less likely it is that reality is transparent to us. Instead one perceives reality in a conditioned, selective manner. Ignorance or 'avidya' is, therefore, not a lack of knowledge but having the wrong kind of knowledge, and about constantly ignoring, underestimating, and altering our perceptions about anything. It is described as spiritual ignorance. The root 'vid' means to exist. And 'avid' means that which does not exist. There is usually a difference between what is and what one thinks it is.

The real Self within, which is simply the ability to perceive, is pure, eternal and without suffering. And due to ignorance one confuses the impure body as being the real Self. And body is not where one can find happiness. Perception that is insightful and that helps in understanding the nature of reality as it is, needs total attention. Only then there is no separation between what we seem to perceive and the actual.

Key words: Afflictions, Mind, Reality

Ego defined

II.6   drug-darshana-shaktyor eka atmata iva asmita

दृक् दर्शन शक्त्योर एक आत्मता इव अस्मिता ।

drk: power of consciousness, the Self within; darshana: perception; shaktyor: ability; eka atmata: in the same manner; iva: as if; asmita: Ego, I-am-ness

Ego is to consider the Self and the power of perceiving to be the same thing.

'Asmi' means 'I am', and 'asmita' means 'I am-this.' The sense of 'I am' is the feeling of the Self as an individual being. It is a common human experience. 'Asmita' is identifying the Self with the body, mind and the intellect. That means mental activity is viewed as the source of perception.

'Asmita' or egoism is the sense of self-importance, and an innate tendency in us all, that eventually brings pain. It then becomes an affliction We link our sensations, thoughts, and possessions to our sense of Self. Growing up we accumulate possessions and develop our own sense of Self based on our thoughts and possessions. Is our identity in our appearance, and our possessions? The Rig Veda (I, 164, 37) says: What thing I am I do not know. I wander alone, burdened by my mind.'

There is nothing more powerful and basic than human identity. Growing up there is a multitude of changing influences on how we think, make our choices, and the times and the cultures we live in. Erickson said: "Identity formation employs a process of simultaneous reflection and observation… The individual judges himself in the light of what he perceives to be the way in which others judge him in comparison to themselves and to a typology significant to them."[1] At the same time, in these times of hyper-individualism, it is worth considering what Robert Penn Warren said: You live through that little piece of time that is yours, but that piece of time is not your only life, it is the summing up of all the other lives that are simultaneous with yours… What you are is an expression of History. Ravindra[2] said: While growing up we inherit certain viewpoints, capabilities that being members of a family, of a society are passed on to us. One becomes part of a web of connections and interactions, and our interests and skills are built upon foundations that we have had little part in forming.

How we view ourselves has a significant bearing on our thoughts, objectives, our interactions. That can be energizing in a positive constructive way and, can also limit our experience. Self-gratification; our possessiveness and apprehensions; together define and motivate us. Self-identity is many times viewed as self-importance. The feeling of self-importance, confines us within our own concerns and priorities.

What is the result of such misidentification? It contributes to selfishness, holding on to what we like and disregard everything else that does not appeal to us when in fact we are part of the whole. It becomes the principal factor affecting all the decisions we make in life. It results in our making choices, creating polarities, such as, this or that, true or false, or like and dislike. The concept of self is constructed and sustained based on these. It is these polarities that separate our basic Self from our built up, changeable, the apparent self, and we ascribe our real Self to that apparent self.

The perceiver in us, according to yoga philosophy, is a spiritual entity called the Purusha. Purusha is the consciousness, awareness within us and, in everyday terms, described as our real Self, or as our soul. It is the power behind all experience. The body, and the mind represent its material counterpart and represent a different kind of energy. While both the spiritual and material aspects are separate, their interaction provides the essential elements in any experience. When there is free and pure vision, we see things as they are. Identifying the material with the spiritual clouds the higher consciousness within us.

Key words: Afflictions, Self

1. Erickson Erik H., 1968. Identity: Youth and Crisis. W.W. Norton and Co., New York.

2. Ravindra Ravi, 1984. Whispers from the other Shore: A Spiritual Search – East and West. A Quest Original, the Theosophical Publishing House, Wheaton, IL.

Attachment

II.7   sukha anushayi ragah

सुख अनुशयी राग: ।

sukha: happiness; anushayi: resulting from, close connection; ragah: love, affection, liking

Attachment stems from (experiences) of happiness.

The third obstacle to Yoga, again like egoism emanating from ignorance, is the affliction of desires and attachments, termed 'raga'. Desire and attachment come from expectation of pleasurable sensations. We derive pleasure from things that may have little to do with survival. Mostly attachments arise because of some physical, emotional or intellectual satisfaction that they provide. Coveting new pleasures can be an optical illusion, indicative of error of perspective. It focuses on one part of reality and forgets the rest.[1] Do objects and experiences really deliver happiness, a life free of suffering for everyone?

One wants to experience old pleasures again in the present and new ones in the future. There are experiences that stay in the form of memories and impressions and the pleasant ones keep urging us to re-experience those. Some desires need to be satisfied to maintain health, nurture the mind and experience the world. But some pleasures can be destructive, causing us harm. Some desires, when repeatedly satisfied, tend to intensify as time goes by. If left unsatisfied they result in restlessness and sometimes even stress; plus, whatever makes us happy does not last. Routine compulsions and addictions, if denied, result in anxious moments that we are usually unaware of. The assumption that anything can provide ever-lasting happiness usually becomes problematic. We all strive to experience what life can offer in terms of pleasure and happiness, but that does not mean ignoring the complex and pain causing reality of life.

Attachments also result in maintaining and deepening ignorance. The root of these tendencies is in the ego, and the ego itself is rooted in ignorance. By associating with the pleasurable sensations one thinks the body and the mind are the Self. Intensified desires manifest in the form of greed and any obstacles in the effort to satisfy that greed leads to anger. Anger leads to illusions and that affects intelligence. Those who can rise above the desire for mundane experiences and objects and help others are spared such effects. Disregard for the welfare of others is neither good nor right. We depend of others as they depend on us.

Key words: Afflictions, Self

1. Ricard Matthieu, Christophe Andre, and Alexandre Jollien, 2018. In Search of Wisdom: A Monk, a Philosopher, and a Psychiatrist on What Matters Most. Sounds True, Boulder, Colorado.

<u>Aversions</u>

II.8   duhkha anusayi dvesha

दु:ख अनुशयी द्वेष: ।

duhkha: pain; anusayi: resulting from; dvesha: dislike

Aversion arises from experiencing suffering.

The flip side of 'raga' is 'dvesha', which represents the opposite experience, of pain. The dichotomy between pleasure and pain, praise and blame, always exists. Our interactions with others frequently cause such opposite emotions. Unsatisfied desires cause unhappiness and can be unsettling. Negative experiences of pain and rejection generate hatred. 'Dvesha' intensifies from simple resentment to envy and hatred, and ultimately brings more grief to the individual, rather than satisfaction In life, many times, we make decisions based on what feels good and what does not. Socio-cultural factors can play a role in whether we perceive something or someone as likable or not, judging the familiar one-way, and unfamiliar the other way. But we may not always know how appropriate these feelings are for our physical and psychological welfare, or how they affect close and functional relationships. Any unpleasant experience limits us as we try to avoid the circumstances, situations and interactions that we associate with suffering. Feelings of hurt tend to cling to our minds. We think about those, nurse the hurt, consider ways of easing the discomfort felt and essentially keep on holding them in our thinking.

We define ourselves in terms of our preferences and experiences. An affliction or 'klesha' is the fear that our sense of self might be altered. And the fear of losing that sense of self becomes a problem. We hate something when the memory of an unpleasant experience reminds us of the past pain. We identify our self with the emotion and that makes it more difficult for us to separate from the hurt. Feelings of hate and anger, therefore, persist and stay fresh while separating us from others, and from the real world.

The answer lies in freeing oneself by nurturing dispassion for displeasure through introspection, through switching to engaging options. It takes understanding and practice to free oneself from the hold of both pleasure and pain. Self-examination of the nature of negative thoughts, our socio-political conditioning and past actions is helpful. Simply identifying an emotional experience can soften our reactive tendencies.

Key words: Affliction, Practice, Self

Fear of Change

II.9   svarasa-vahi vidusah api tatha arudho abhinivesah

स्वरसवाही विदुष: अपि तथा अरुठ अभिनिवेश: ।

svarasa: love of life; vahi: current; vidusah: learned; api:
even; tatha: in that way; arudha: dominating; abhinivesah:
fear of death, of change

Self-preservation or attachment to life is found in everyone, even
in the wise.

'Abhinivesha' is described as fear of death and all beings
feel that. Love for life and self-preservation are instinctive tendencies. The fear of death is unlearnt and untaught, and even the
learned are not immune to its hold. According to the concept of
reincarnation that fear is carried over from one life to the next.
Irrespective of where it comes from, it is natural for us all. Existential fear is a basic emotion and it arises from identification with
the body, which is non-permanent. We value self-perpetuation.
There is always the fear of facing uncertainty and of not having
control over what happens around and to us. Once we are born
and the Self, the basic awareness within connects with the material world, attachment to life, as we know it, self-sustains till the
end.

'Abhinivesha' is better described as fear of change, and as
a wish to continue with things as they are. A likelihood of change
means uncertainty regarding what is next. And that is uncomfortable given that one develops some ease with things known to us.
At the same time, not all changes are undesirable. Changes
mean new opportunities and altered states that can be energizing
and rewarding in various ways. Staying the course is important
for attaining goals. A lifelong discipline of staying aware of such
differences and accepting the inevitability of change is a better
approach to life.

Overcoming attachment to life and resistance to change depends on developing an intuitive understanding of what we are, and how our life experiences evolve. We have limited control over changes around and within us. Attachments and aversions constitute an important part of our idea of what we are and while they condition and channel our choices, the ability to let go of those is an important part of finding relief from the grievances of life. Understanding the multiple ever-changing dimensions of experiences is crucial for that.

Intellectually one may accept the inevitability of change. But understanding and coping with such knowledge requires wisdom. The solution for overcoming any existential fears lies in strengthening the ability to dissociate from the status quo. It does not come easily and depends on a continuing attention towards resisting the lures and comforts of the known, while also staying open to the unknown.

Key words: Afflictions, Reality, Self

Sutras 10-17 are about cultivating the ability to monitor thoughts and actions through the practice of focusing on opposite feelings.

<u>Reversal of attention</u>

II.10 te pratiprasava-heyah suksmah

ते प्रतिप्रसव हेया: सूक्ष्मा: ।

te: they; pratiprasava: counter-flow; heyah: to be overcome; suksmah: subtle

Subtle afflictions are to be minimized and eradicated by a process of turning inwards.

Our natural tendency from the very beginning of life is to reach out to the world. In that process, we condition our mind to accept what appeals and reject what does not. That conditioning means misinterpreting reality, personalizing and limiting experiences, with a view to keep a continuous investment in self-perpetuation. Afflictions are bound with the body/mind. Mostly they lie dormant, stay intermittently active, are weak or are fully activated. Only at birth, or upon attainment of the pinnacle state of meditative absorption wherein discriminative intelligence is attained (as in 'asamprajnata' Samadhi), are those afflictions rendered inoperative. 'Pratiprasava' is return to the original state of unaffectedness.

With focused attention, any negative experience can be subjected to a scrutiny. One can look at its moment by moment evolution, and the sensations that accompanied and followed it. One can evaluate and examine it, and the action that one may wish to or may have taken in response. It is becoming aware of the multiple dimensions of unwelcome experiences. Negation is a Vedanta practice. The terms neti, neti, mean not this, not this. It is a process of removing, negating what anything is purported to be. For example, one removes or separates what a certain feeling, such as love, is, from what it is not.

This is followed by thinking about the opposite of any negative thought. Thus, the opposite of arrogance is humility; of greediness, it is restraint. 'Pratiprasava' is the name for this technique and a way out of the five afflictions, the 'kleshas', described in the earlier Sutras. By following it one can return to the non-afflicted state one is born with. The focus is on welcoming and nurturing positive feelings. When we extend a friendly hand, we cannot make a fist at the same time. By bringing in positive thoughts we can edge out the negative ones. Bringing one face to face one's hatreds and desires exposes asmita, I-am-ness, and weakens 'abhinivesha', the desire to continue. The practice is to think about and nurture what the opposite of a certain negative thought is. The Rig Veda says (I-89-i): Let noble thoughts come to us from every side.

Positive thinking can have powerful effects. It depends on the individual to use that power effectively. This is where a strong base of ethics plays an important role. Patanjali's inclusion of the ethical norms and personal restraints (to be described later) is an important part of the overall yogic practices.

Key words: Attention, Afflictions, Mind

<u>Meditation</u>

II.11 dhyana-heyas tad-vrttayah

ध्यान हेयास तद वृत्तय: ।

dhyana: meditation; heyas: to be avoided; tad-vrttayah: their activities

The suffering due to afflictions is silenced by meditation.

In life we face various imbalances and unwelcome experiences caused mostly by our afflicted ways of thinking. Patanjali recommends meditation to reduce the effects of afflictions that limit our understanding. Meditation brings about reversal in the outward flow of the common tendencies of the mind, described in the previous Sutra. The objective of meditation is to discover the reasons for our suffering so that we can work at finding ways to address that. That depends on our understanding of experiences, the subtle influences of our built-up self, with its likes, dislikes and fears, that we cannot let go off, and the causes thereof. 'Svadhyaya', the introspective meditative process, is an important practice aimed at reversing the flow of attention from the outward and superficial, to the inward and meaningful. By knowing our inner worlds, feelings and emotions, plus our interpersonal relationships and life in our communities, we establish a balance within varied aspects of our life and such balance establishes peace.

By meditating, we self-transform from within. Introspection is a disciplined process. It is about taking an in-depth look at experiences and how to interpret what those mean. The first step in meditation is dissociating from multiple interests and bringing attention towards a single place. Next comes practicing meditation either by focusing on an object, a thought or an activity. When the attention is so focused one realizes the multiple facets of the object of focus, including noticing changes in that. Such attention is helpful in overcoming the mind's tendency to wander. When the attention is focused on a thought, reflection on the thought in the context of life's deeper problems is helpful in deconstructing it. Examination of how the afflictions assert their hold on thoughts and actions is part of such discipline. It is about overcoming suffering, quieting the mind, and finding ways to clear its afflictions.

Key words: Attention, Afflictions, Mind, Practice

Actions and karma

II.12 klesha mulah karmasayah drsta adrsta janma vedaniyah

क्लेश मूल: कर्म आशय: द्रुष्ट अद्रुष्ट जन्म वेदनीय: ।

klesha: affliction; mulah: root; karmasayah: reservoir of karma; drsta: seen; adrsta: unseen; janma: lives; vedaniyah: to be experienced

The impressions of past actions, stored deep in the mind, are the triggers behind actions. Under appropriate conditions they appear in similar actions in seen and unseen ways – in this life, or in a future one.

Our actions, good or bad, leave imprints, called 'samskaras'. These imprints accumulate in the conscious as well as subconscious mind as we go through life and become our set-in tendencies. The imprints are like seeds that germinate and bring rewards if the actions are good, or result in suffering if the actions are hurtful to others. Pools of positive/negative effects, called karma, due to good/bad actions build up. The seeds that do not so germinate retain their potential to re-emerge later, sometimes through the next birth-cycle.

When the actions are free of any limitations due to afflic-tions ('klesha') they tend not to leave any imprints. Therefore, by acting judiciously, not succumbing to the pull of desires, greed, pride, anger, or malice, the size of the pool of imprints can be kept limited. In addition, following Kriya Yoga practices (see Sutra II.1) also helps clear up the reservoir of negative karma.

Key words: Mind

<u>Karma consequences</u>

II.13 sati mule tadvipkah jati ayuh bhogah

सति मूले तद् विपाक: जाति आयु: भोग: ।

sati: there being; mule: the root; tad: its; vipakah: ripening;

jati: class; ayuh: life span; bhogah: experiences

The dormant roots of actions reveal in the quality of birth, of experiences and span of life.

All afflicted actions leave imprints that become the seeds for future actions. While some imprints may not stay in our consciousness, others can remain in the subconscious. Not all such seeds bear fruit immediately; they remain dormant and germinate only under appropriate conditions. The nature of such dormant seeds, whether pleasant or harmful, determines a range of possible, pleasing or hurtful, consequences.

Thoughts affect actions. Therefore, it becomes important to fully understand our thoughts, and how they affect our actions. Understanding our desires and fears empowers us. By exercising judgment and being selective about actions to be undertaken, we can limit suffering in life.

Key words: Afflictions, Mind

<u>Karma consequences – cont.</u>

II.14 te hlada paritapa phalah punya apunya hetutvat

ते ल्हाद परिताप फल: पुण्य अपुण्य हेतुत्वात् ।

te: they; hlada: joy; paritapa: and sorrow; phalah: fruit; punya: merit; apunya: sin; hetutvat: because of

Our actions determine whether we have a long or short life, and whether it is happy or unhappy.

This Sutra reiterates how the law of Karma operates throughout life. Afflictions caused by ignorance and feelings of self-importance produce actions that have consequences. These are expressed in the form of the type of life we are born to, its span, and whether our life experiences are pleasant or painful. Our choices matter in how we think and what actions we take. Pleasing experiences bind us by keeping us motivated to repeat the type of actions that initially brought pleasure. A cycle of actions and expected pleasures eventually results in pain and anguish and is unsustainable.

A disciplined way of life and mindfulness regarding the implications of our choices matter in deciding whether our life experiences are joyful or whether they lead to sorrow. Disciplined and judicious actions prevent unwelcome experiences.

Key words: Afflictions, Practice

<u>Dealing with changes</u>

II.15 parinama-tapa-samskara-duhkair guna-vrtti-virodhat ca duhkham-eva sarvam vivekinah

परिणाम ताप संस्कार दु:खै: गुण वृत्ति विरोधाच्च दु:खम् एव सर्वम् विवेकिन: ।

parinama: because of; tapa: suffering; samskara: impression; duhkair: pains; guna: qualities;

vrtti: modifications; virodhat: because of opposition; ca: and; duhkham: pain; eva: only; sarvam: all; vivekinah: to the wise;

Only the wise know that due to changes, inherent tendencies in nature, and subliminal impressions, even pleasant experiences are tinged with sorrow. They therefore stay aloof of them.

This Sutra is about the causes and effects of changes around us and how to deal with them. The constant ongoing changes in the world around us cause suffering. Superficially pleasant and eventually grief producing thoughts and experiences resulting from relentless changes are referred to as 'parinama' in this Sutra. These keep occurring. Our natural reaction to change is apprehension, anxiety and fear. We feel secure in holding on to status quo. Given that nothing lasts, our efforts to hold on to a status quo ultimately fail. Neither can we ignore changes. Either way there is suffering (tapa).

Changes are due to the changing balance of energies ('guna': See Sutra I.16) within us and in the world around us. We find some changes appealing and some that are unsettling. While one feels drawn to pleasure bringing changes, it is the unsettling changes that cause stress, bring discomfort and sometimes misery. It takes wisdom to handle the pull of short lived pleasures and strength to cope with stress and anxiety.

We are prone to repeating certain type of actions. Actions leave impressions, called 'samskara' (See Sutra I.11). 'Samskara' are like grooves in how we think and they bind us to repeating the actions that caused them in the first place. Adhering to the same options in the face of changed circumstances leads to imbalance and anxiety.

Freedom from pain requires transformation of our ordinary tendencies. That freedom comes with introspection. It is instrumental in resisting the pull of reactive tendencies and stress producing habitual ways. Thoughts and actions, are paramount in determining whether life experiences are pleasant or painful. Accepting, adjusting and reevaluating responses is the less painful option in such circumstances. The pleasures derived from fulfilled desires are never lasting and are many times illusory. For freeing oneself from suffering we need to be aware of the ongoing changes and how they affect us. And one needs to have discriminating intelligence for that. When we are aware of the conditions that narrow our understanding, and limit our perceptions, it helps us in facing changes and their effects, and in working at overcoming them. Once the determination comes, then we can work with our mind and find appropriate behavioral strategies towards developing positive options.

Key words: Afflictions, Mind, Practice

<u>Pain is avoidable</u>

II.16   heyam duhhkam anagatam

हेयं दु:खम् अनागतम् ।

heyam: to be avoided; duhhkam: misery; anagatam: future

Future suffering can be avoided.

This Sutra, on an optimistic note, points out that there is a way out of suffering due to indecision, anguish, or compulsive behaviors, and the constant search for pleasure. The future pain is not inevitable. Past suffering is erased and current suffering, the result of previous causes, can be lessened through Yoga practices. The present bears the seeds that eventually cause suffering in the future and that can be avoided. The mind plays an important role in this and the answer lies in transforming our ingrained ways of thinking and compulsive ways of behaving. The previous as well as the subsequent Sutras refer to the various ways in which this can be achieved.

Meditation is a distancing practice. It allows the Self, our innate awareness, to view and examine the mind's ongoing movements as an observer. One can then assess and evaluate the true nature of incoming experiences. This empowers the mind to prevent making rash decisions and take hasty actions. All actions, when evaluated, help uncondition perceptions and this makes decision-making more balanced.

Key words: Afflictions, Mind, Practice

<u>Separate the 'seer' from the 'seen'.</u>

II.17 drastr drsyayoh samyogo heya hetuh

द्रष्टृ द्रश्ययो: संयोगो हेय हेतु: ।

drastr: of Self; drsyayoh: seen; samyogo: union; heya: that which is to be avoided; hetuh: cause

The cause of pain is the identification of the Self with the seen and the remedy for that lies in their dissociation.

We associate our Self to be what we see and experience, when in fact we as 'seers' are separate from what we see and experience. There is an intermittent contact between us and any experience, or object, and until then they remain as separate entities. For objects to be seen there needs to be a 'seer'. Without the 'seer' the objects remain unrecognized and unseen. And considering the 'seer' and its object to be the same is misidentifying the seen with the 'seer'. And that is the reason for our suffering.

Who is the 'seer', the 'knower'? It is not the body, that senses. Neither is it our conscious mind, that perceives. These are affected by our superficial perceptions of what we are and conditioned by our changing likes, dislikes and fears. The 'seer' is the basic unaffected and unencumbered awareness, the Self, within us. The 'seen' or the known includes the body, the mind and the world around us. Not realizing the difference between the Self and the 'seen' results in our immersing indiscriminately into the material world. That ultimately results in pain.

The desire for sampling worldly pleasures can result in our tendency to overdo and that results in loss of inner harmony. Inaction or resisting pain is also unsettling. We seek equanimity and balance. Peace is found in distancing awareness from the objective world. For a correct understanding of reality, self-knowledge, and to make appropriate choices one needs discriminating intelligence, free of the hold of the sensory mind. This intelligence has a serene quality and it is close to our innate awareness that is reflected in it, while still, remaining separate from it. Realization of this separateness between the 'seer' and the 'seen' clears suffering.

Key words: Mind, Self

Sutras 18-25 are about the twin aspects of reality, the Self within and the world without.

Changing balance of energies in all objects

II.18 prakasa-kriya-sthiti-silam bhuta indriya atmakam bhoga apavarga artham drsyam

प्रकाश क्रिया स्थिति शीलम् भूत इन्द्रिय आत्मकम् भोग आपवर्ग अर्थम् द्रुश्यम् ।

prakasa: luminosity; kriya: activity; sthiti: stability; silam: having the qualities of; bhut: elements; indriya: sense-organs; atmakam: being of the nature; bhog: experience; apavargartham: liberation; drsyam: seen

That which is knowable, the 'seen', has the qualities ('guna') of illumination, activity, and inertia ('sattva', 'rajas' and 'tamas'). The 'seen' consists of the senses and the elements, and exists for (providing) experience and liberation.

This Sutra describes the nature of the objective world. The form and state of any object is the result of the balance among the three 'gunas' (described as energies, tendencies, qualities) namely, 'rajas', 'tamas' and 'sattva'. 'Rajas' is active energy, 'tamas' is inertia, and 'sattva' represents the cognitive or illuminative quality. 'Sattva' is the state of equilibrium without positive or negative agitation. Prakriti's tendency is to seek this state.

Perception involves interaction between objects and the body, and the mind. There is a dynamic balance among the three qualities in all objects, including our body, the mind that perceives and interprets. However, the shifting balance within the three energies changes both the perceiving mind as well as what it perceives. The objects are for providing enjoyment, and experiences while they can also help us liberate us from suffering in life. Normally our intelligence is tainted and darkened by the active or passive nature of the senses and the elements. When cleared of these, the separate identities of our basic awareness, which is the Self, or the 'seer', vs. the 'seen' (i.e., everything material, the body and the mind) are revealed. There is liberation from confusion, tension and conflict, if one does not indiscriminately pursue sense experiences.

Key words: Mind, Reality, Self

More on the Gunas

II.19 visesa avisesa lingamatra alingani guna-parvani

विशेष अविशेष लिंगमात्र अलिंगानि गुण पर्वाणि ।

visesa: specific; avisesa: non-specific; lingamatra: mark; alingani: without mark; guna: qualities; parvani: states, levels

Everything consists of gunas, the fundamental qualities of nature. They operate at gross, subtle, and unmanifest levels.

The phenomenal world or Prakriti before creation, is unde-fined until it manifests as the material world of objects. There are definable/identifiable and undefinable/unidentifiable states of these. Material objects appear in the form of five inorganic ele-ments; namely earth, water, air, space and energy. These are combined in varying proportions in everything. Their gross forms are manifest, while the subtle forms may remain hidden. In all objects, initially, the three 'Gunas' (refer to the previous Sutra) are in perfect balance. Once created, the manifestations of mate-rial objects, change due to shifting balances among the three en-ergies or qualities.

The cosmic intelligence is a counterpart of the phenomenal world. The cosmic intelligence, the subtle world of conscious-ness, is also undefinable. The 'I', or the 'Self' is the individual part of the cosmic intelligence. It is indiscernible.

The instrument of the Self, the mind is, like the phenomenal world, subject to the shifting balance among the three energies. Our consciousness consists of the mind complex, chitta, that in-cludes the intellect, the sensory mind that receives the sense inputs, and the ego as its interpreter. Our perceptions and thoughts are distinct phenomena and these are individualized.

Most objects remain invisible to the senses. We connect with some of those through our senses; taste, smell, shape, touch and sound. For example, the element of air is associated with sound. Here, the knowledge of sound ('sattva') is the result of the motion in air ('rajas') and the intervening gaps represent the inertia ('tamas') energies. We hear the vibrations produced by sound.

Key words: Mind, Reality, Self

The 'seer' is the witness

II.20 drsta drsmatrah suddhah api pratyaya anupasyah

द्रष्टा द्रुशिमात्र: शुघ्द: अपि प्रत्यय अनुपश्य: ।

drsta: Self, the 'seer'; drsmatrah: pure consciousness only; suddhah: pure; api: though; pratyaya: concept;

anupasyah: appears to see along with

The Self is pure consciousness. It illumines contents of the mind.

The Self, or the soul, interacts with the world using the intellect, the I-maker, and the sensory mind. However, all these (the mind complex of intellect/I-maker/sensory mind) constitute simply the Self's proxy and not the Self herself. The mind complex presents the perceptions to the Self and mistakenly considers itself to be the Self or the soul. Its function is simply to bring the world experience to the Self, the pure awareness within. The Self is the witness and not the active participant in the act of perceiving.

The mind, being subject to the dynamism in the energies within, is constantly changing whereas the soul, the Self remains unchanged. Just as less than transparent instruments cannot provide a clear vision, our ever-changing perceptions do not represent a clear or complete picture of the phenomenal world. Until the discerning intelligence can clear the intermediate filters, the true form of perceptions does not reach the soul or the Self. Perceptions that the Self receives are incomplete and unclear as a result. Just as the reflection of the sun or the moon in turbulent waters is far from clear, the perceptions that the conditioned mind conveys are inaccurate.

Key words: Mind, Reality, Self

The 'seen' serves the 'seer'

II.21   tad-artha eva drsyasya atma

तद् अर्थ एव दृश्यस्य आत्मा ।

tad: that; artha: purpose; eva: alone; drsyasya: of the seen; atma: being, soul

The purpose of the seen is only to serve the Self, the seer.

The phenomenal world exists to serve the awareness, the 'seer' or the Self within us. It has no other purpose. Intelligence, the senses, the organs of action, all interact with the world around and present the picture of the world to the Self. The world is for the Self, to experience. In that process, the Self gets entangled into it, drawn in by the afflicted mind instrument. But when the perceptions are freed of their limitations through various Yoga practices, and actions are judiciously undertaken, the Self is liberated from that entanglement.

Key words: Reality, Self

<u>Freedom from the material world</u>

II.22 krata artham prati nastam apy anastam tad anya

sadharanatvat

कृत अर्थम् प्रति नष्टम् अप्य अनष्टम् तत् अन्य साधारणत्वात् ।

krata: accomplished; artha: purpose; prati: for; nastam: destroyed; apy: although; anastam: not destroyed; tad: that; anya: to others; sadharanatvat: for being common

For liberated beings, nature becomes irrelevant, since its purpose has been fulfilled. But its processes continue to affect others.

Once the practitioner is liberated and free of the influence of changing states of experiences, the phenomenal world ceases to be relevant. Apart from satisfying basic existential needs, that practitioner has no desires, no aversions, and no fears. For her, existence is insightful. Experiences continue from one to the next and do not leave any lasting impressions.

As for the others, nature's changing states continue to affect them, leaving impressions on their minds, subjecting them to the consequences thereof. The interaction between individual aware-ness and nature remains their reality. The sole purpose of the enlightened is to assist such persons in finding relief from suffer-ing.

Key words: Reality, Wisdom

<u>The 'seer' and the 'seen' are separate entities.</u>

II.23 sva-svami-saktyoh sva-rupa-upalabdhi-hetuh samyogah

स्व स्वामि शक्त्यो: स्वरूप उपलब्धि हेतु: संयोग: ।

sva: its; svami: master; sakti: power; svarup: own form; upalabdhi: knowledge; hetuh: cause; samyogah: union, conjunction, confusion

When the 'seer' and the 'seen' become one, it brings realization of the true nature of each and understanding of their real functions.

The interaction between the 'seer', or the Self and the 'seen' is for the 'seer' to realize her own nature and for experiencing the unfolding nature of the 'seen'. The two are far from being the same. In the conjunction between the two, the awareness, by itself, remains unchanged. But the world around, the 'seen', including the body and mind keep changing.

The, awareness within, the 'Self, is there to simply observe. And the function of the mind is to deliver experience. We mistakenly think that the mind is the Self and this misidentification limits our understanding of the world and is the cause of suffering in life. The ability to cognize and correct the limitations of the mind eases suffering and opens the multiple dimensions of all observed and experienced phenomena available to the Self within us. It is then that one truly sees the difference between these two entities.

Key words: Reality, Self

<u>Misperception is due to ignorance</u>

II.24 tasya hetuh avidya

तस्य हेतु: अविद्या ।

tasya: its; hetuh: cause; avidya: ignorance

The cause of conjunction of Self with the seen is ignorance about their real nature.

Our shifting experiences of suffering and happiness are due to our ignorance regarding the true relationship between the Self (the awareness within us) and the 'seen' (objects and experiences). Our perceptions focus on fragments of the whole and that limits our knowledge and understanding of the big picture. Until that ignorance is removed and the separation between the seeing entity and the seen material is understood, suffering persists. The Self remains confined to the hold of the phenomenal world. The mind experiences confusion, lacks objectivity and has mistaken understanding about its nature. When that hold is released and ignorance is cleared by attaining discriminatory intelligence, one sees things clearly and as they are, and these are delivered to the Self.

Key words: Reality, Self

<u>Dissociation between the 'seer' and the 'seen' is liberation.</u>

II.25 tat-abhavat samyogah abhavah hanam tad-drseh
kaivalyam

तत् अभावात् संयोग: अभाव: हानम् तत् द्रशे: कैवल्यम् ।

tat: of that; abhavat: without; samyoga: union, association; abhavo: disappearance; hanam: avoidance; tat: that; drseh: of the seer; kaivalyam: liberation

When ignorance is destroyed through right knowledge, the Self (the 'seer') is liberated from its identification with the world as seen or experienced. This liberation is enlightenment.

The mind, part of the 'seen', connects the Self within us to the pleasures and, also to the disappointments, that inevitably follow unfulfilled desires. We believe the mind to be who we are, when in fact our awareness is what we are. That awareness is the Self, our soul. Our ignorance about things makes us susceptible to suffering in life. What prevents this from happening is judicious thinking. It takes diligent practice towards distancing from distracting choices to develop and nurture such thinking. When the connection between the 'seen' and the Self is severed, the imbalances and suffering that are part of experiencing the 'seen' end. This frees the Self.

Kaivalya or release from Prakriti is considered as the ideal in life according to the Sankhya-yoga philosophy. In the Upanishadic yoga, the individual self ultimately unites with the universal, absolute self, whereas in this yoga the self extricates itself from Prakriti. So, in the Upanishadic yoga it is meant as 'union' whereas in Sankhya yoga it means 'disunion' or viyoga.

Key words: Practice, Reality, Self

Sutras 26-29 refer to the first five of the eight limbs of Patanjali Yoga.

Wisdom for clearing confusion

II.26 viveka-khyatih aviplava hana-upayah

विवेक ख्याति: अविप्लवा हान उपाय: ।

viveka: judgment; khyatih: awareness; aviplava: clarity; hana: removal, upayah: means, method

Steady vision of discernment (viveka) is the way to overcome ignorance.

We tend to live in the state of ignorance and are unaware of the true nature of our Self and of the material world that delivers the world experience to the Self. That affects how we think and behave. The distorted view of reality results in confusion and discomfort. The mind stays in a state of disorder and chaos, unable to know the real from the illusion. There are many layers of understanding within our inner world and to become aware of those worlds we need to withhold extraneous influences from intruding. Questioning and seeking the reasons for extraneous influences can transform our thinking and behaviors. Observation of our own behaviors provides the foundation for that.

Meditation is a way of doing such observation and examination. It is a means for witnessing movements in consciousness. Simply being aware, without correcting anything, merely observing the happenings can initially provide a sense of order. That helps purify the psyche by ridding psychological conditioning. In the deep state of concentration one is more likely to see the big picture. One realizes that using judgment in thinking and speaking, and discriminative knowledge in performing any actions, results in calming the wandering mind. When wisdom arrives, ignorance departs.

Key words: Afflictions, Mind, Practice

Progression of wisdom

II.27 tasya saptdha pranta-bhumih prajna

तस्य सप्तधा प्रान्त भूमि: प्रज्ञा ।

tasya: his; saptdha: sevenfold; pranta: last; bhumih: stage; prajna: wisdom

Unbroken flow of discriminative awareness or wisdom evolves through seven stages. Then it ushers in enlightenment.

This Sutra has been interpreted differently by different commentators. In general, awareness of the movements of the body and of the mind helps guide one towards exercising the appropriate restraints in behavior. By nurturing one-pointedness the mind is becalmed, and self-knowledge attained. There is clarity and peace when the ego is weakened and the multiple dimensions of reality are discerned. The unbroken flow of awareness referred to in this Sutra is referring to the successively deeper absorption levels attained in meditation.

Following the first seven of eight limbs of the Yogic endeavor leads to unfolding of different aspects of the body/mind apparatus. Once accomplished, the eighth limb, Samadhi, illuminates the whole spectrum of human life and its existential relationship with the objective world. That special wisdom is called 'prajna', meaning deep insight.

Key words: Practice, Wisdom

Wisdom through practice

II.28 yoga-anga-anusthanat asuddhi-ksaye jnana-diptih a viveka-kyateh

योगांग अनुष्ठानात् अशुद्धि क्षय ज्ञान दिप्ति: अविवेक ख्याते: ।

yogang: part of Yoga; anusthanad: by devoted practice; asuddhi: impurity; ksaya: destruction; jnana: knowledge; diptih: light; a: up to; viveka: wisdom, discriminative knowledge; kyateh: attainment

Yoga practices, done with dedication, destroy impurities; and that brings radiating wisdom.

The very first Sutra in Chapter I addresses the interested student to follow the Yoga discipline, which is a practice, subject to a set of rules, and has a disciplined code of conduct and precepts. This Sutra describes the benefits that accrue as a result. The yogic way of living is based on developing the type of discerning intelligence described in the previous Sutra II.27. An undistorted view of reality is gained due to the ability to distinguish between what is fact based and what is wishful, and the permanent from the changing. A conditioned worldview is fragmentary and ultimately results in conflict and confusion.

There are various obstacles (the five afflictions ('kleshas') described Sutras II.3-9) in the path towards achieving a tranquil mind and a regular and consistent practice of yoga helps in removing those. When the various Yoga practices (introduced in the next Sutra) are regularly done with devotion, the impurities of the body and mind are cleansed. Wisdom dawns as the causes of afflictions are removed and physical, mental, and spiritual, suffering is overcome. Ramana Maharshi[1] (1879-1950) said: The jnani (the wise) weeps with the weeping, laughs with the laughing, plays with the playful. Sings with those who sing. The jnani is the mirror but unaffected by the image. The jnani is like a child. Incidents interest a child only so long as they last. It ceases to think of them after they have passed away. They do not leave any impressions.

Key words: Afflictions, Wisdom

1. Ramana Maharishi, 1985. Be as You Are: The Teachings of Sri Ramana Maharshi. Edited by David Godman, Penguin Books.

<u>What is Ashtanga Yoga</u>

II.29 yama-niyama asana pranayama pratyahara dharana
dhyana samadhayah astau angani

यम नियम आसन प्राणायाम प्रत्याहार धारणा ध्यान समाधय: अष्ट
अंगानि ।

yama: self-restraints; niyam: self-disciplines; asana:
posture; pranayama: breath regulation; pratyahara:
withdrawal; dharana: concentration; dhyana: meditation;
samadhayah: total absorption; astau: eight; angani: limbs

Self-restraints, self-disciplines, posture, regulation of breath,
sense control, concentration, meditation, and total absorption are
the eight practices of Yoga.

In this Sutra Patanjali presents his eight-part system of
Yoga. He refers to these parts as limbs, suggesting that together
they make a functioning system. The first two components of this
eight-limbed Yoga system are related to our interactions with the
world around us and about cultivating certain self-disciplines.
These focus on cultivation of selflessness through introspection
and contemplation, while actively participating in life. They bring
about self-knowledge. The next three practices, namely posture,
breathing and sense withdrawal, focus on the body, its energy
flows, and the senses that interact with the environment. The organs have the tendency to move out towards the objects of enjoyment, such as food or entertainment. This draws the mind
outwards towards them. Pratyahara is the intentional reversal of
this process. Instead of the sense organ pulling the mind, the
mind pulls away from objects the senses are drawn to. The remaining three practices are focused on cultivating progressively
deeper levels of concentration.

All the practices in the eight-part system are interlinked and interdependent and support each other. They represent the progressive development of attention narrowing from the external to the internal worlds where we live. In that process, one remains an active participant in life while bolstering one's bodily and mental preparedness, and maintaining spiritual ease. With increased awareness and discerning intelligence about life experiences one can realize what it really means to have a life free of suffering.

Details about these practices follow in the Sutras below.

Key word: Practice

Sutras 30-55 elaborate on the practices related to the first five limbs in Patanjali's Ashtanga Yoga

<u>The five self-restraints</u>

II.30 ahimsa satya asteya brahmacharya aparigraha yamah

अहिंसा सत्य अस्तेय ब्रह्मचर्य अपरिग्रह यमा: ।

ahimsa: harmless-ness; satya: truthfulness; asteya: honesty; brahmacharya: continence, restraint; aparigraha: non-possessiveness; yamah: self-restraints, virtues

The five self-restraints: abstention from violence, from falsehood, honesty, continence, and non-acquisitiveness are called Yama.

The self-restraints are about our social interactions. They are about refraining from certain types of thoughts and actions. The first mentioned restraint is usually considered the most important one. Thus, refraining from violence is the most important restraint regarding how we interact with and treat others. Accordingly, for maintaining social harmony, violence in any form is to be avoided by the practitioner. That means in all interactions, the feelings, actions, possessions, self-respect of others, are to be left unharmed and undiminished. Intent matters, since if there is no intent to do any harm, for example as in, accidently stepping on an insect, it is not considered violence.

Adhering to truthfulness is another practice that prevents harm to others. It clears false impressions and facilitates cooperation with others. When telling truth hurts the other, it is advisable to stay silent.

Stealing or appropriating something that belongs to others is also harmful to all. First, it deprives the other of a possession and instead of yielding any satisfaction to one who steals it, it feeds insecurity and is ultimately costly to hold on to.

Next, it is important to curb our natural impulses and desires that may result in actions that seem to satisfy and yield pleasure. In all social interactions using appropriate restraints in sexual matters, in how we communicate with others, is crucial. It prevents injury or harm to others.

And last, containing greed is necessary for preventing a chain of negative effects caused in the process of pursuing pleasures and acquiring possessions. Greed leads to and leaves damaging effects on others and their resources. Containing acquisitiveness ultimately helps safeguard resources for all and prevents adverse impacts on others through their use.

All the five restraints above are about respecting others as well as the self, whether it is the truth, the body/feelings, possessions, or desires. While following them is especially deemed imperative for Yoga practitioners; in any situation, as the following Sutra suggests, use of appropriate judgment is advised.

Key words: Ethics, Practice

<u>Adhering to the self-restraints</u>

II.31   jati desa kala samaya anavacchinnah sarva-bhauma mahavratam

जाति देश काल समय अनवच्छिन्ना: सर्वभौमा महाव्रतम् ।

jati: class; desa: place; kala: time; samay: occasion; anavacchinnah: unconditioned; sarvabhauma: universal; mahavratam: great vow

The five vows are not conditioned by time, place, class, or occasion and are universal.

The self-restraints, or moral principles, mentioned in the previous Sutra are referred to as great vows that are universally applicable. This Sutra is about following these. A practitioner needs to always keep those in mind, irrespective of whether one is engaged in routine activities or practicing asana.

Opinions defer regarding how rigorously and literally these restraints are to be observed and followed. Strict adherence can strengthen the resolve and commitment to following the discipline. On the other hand, one may say that following these is about living skillfully. Skillfulness includes correctly evaluating each situation and following humane and practical paths. Rigidity in applying the injunctions can mean unnecessary strife and un-realistic expectations about human behaviors. Just as a fisher-man cannot avoid harming the fish or the warrior the enemy, situ-ations sometimes necessitate overruling these injunctions by varying degrees. Occasional exception may be more conducive to respecting circumstantial and situational prerogatives. The answer lies in seeking an intelligent balance based on self-assessment of the strength of one's own commitment and the imperatives of respecting the demands of place and time. And that would still not be counter to Indian philosophical thought as indicated in the following verse by Manu (4.138)

The truth should be spoken

That which is pleasant should be spoken

That which is truthful but unpleasant should not be uttered

Pleasant but untrue should not be spoken

This is eternal righteousness.

Key words: Ethics, Practice

The five self-disciplines

II.32 sauca santosha tapah svadhyaya Ishwar pranidhanani
niyamah

शौच संतोष तप: स्वाध्याय ईश्वर प्रणिधानानि नियम: ।

sauca: purity; santosha: contentment; tapah: intense effort; svadhyaya: self-study; Ishwar: God; pranidhanani: surrender to; niyamah: self-discipline

Purity, contentment, dedicated effort, self-study, and surrender to God constitute the self-disciplines.

There are five disciplines or practices that are about preparing the practitioner for the Yogic endeavor. Each practice, among the five listed here, prepares the practitioner for the remaining four. The first important one is about maintaining purity of the body and of the mind. Routine purification of the body sets up the intention for following the practice, while proper foods maintain health. BKS Iyengar said: Asana practice cleanses internally by nourishing the body and by removing toxins and impurities. Breathing practices cleanse and aerate lungs.[1] The blood is oxygenated and nerves are becalmed. Mental purity consists of the mind that is free of hostility, anger and distracting thoughts. This is helpful in focusing attention.

Next, staying contented weakens the pull of desires and controls greed, and that keeps one's attention strong and steadfast. Contentedness is not about passively accepting things as they are, but about setting judicious boundaries. Self-discipline applied to the body and the mind prepares the practitioner for practicing contentedness.

The last three, namely self-study, dedicated effort, and surrender to God constitute Kriya Yoga, or the Yoga of Action, referred to in the beginning of this chapter. These three practices are interdependent. The intense effort mentioned in this Sutra is about the importance of will power in maintaining practice, despite other distractions and mundane difficulties. Self-study is monitoring and examining one's own thoughts and actions and studying scriptures for guidance. And last, surrendering to a higher principle, or God, weakens ego and nurtures humility.

Key words: Mind, Practice

1. Iyengar, B.K.S., 1993. Light on the Yoga Sutras of Patanjali. Harper Collins Pub. New Delhi.

Countering negative thinking

II.33 vitarka badhane pratipaksha bhavanam

वि तर्क बाधने प्रतिपक्ष भावनम् ।

vitark: evil thoughts, badhane: painful; pratipaksha: opposite; bhavanam: feeling

When disturbed by negative thoughts, the opposite, positive ones should be nurtured.

There are always some unwholesome and disturbing thoughts that cross our minds. For example, we may wish to harm someone who has hurt us. Yet we condone similar behavior from someone who is dear to us. There is anger at any obstruction, or we may seek control on what we wish to have, or do. Examples of negative emotions are, violence, falsehood, stealing, and faithlessness. These can have different intensities, from being weak to strong, to intense urges. Ultimately, they bring us grief and pain. Besides, they go against the ethical norms and self-disciplines listed in Sutras II.30-32.

The effective technique for countering these, Patanjali recommends, is called pratiprasava. It involves, first, locating the source of, and understanding the evolution of, any negative thought. This is where introspective self-study becomes important. It is important to practice identifying negative emotions. To avoid and manage pain and grief caused by negative thinking, the option is not to suppress that, but to switch attention towards better, more wholesome thoughts. Replacing those by cultivating wholesome emotions relieves the tension negative thinking brings. This is pratiprasava or the reversal of the outward tendencies, and furthering inward tendencies.

Paksha bhavanah are positive emotions such as, purity, contentment, having faith, humility, and flexibility. Wholesome thoughts can neutralize pain-causing urges and tendencies. Matthieu Ricard says: We can get rid of thoughts that trouble us by calling up thoughts that are diametrically opposed to them; kindness vs. hate, patience vs. irritation, and so on. A thought of love and a thought of hate cannot exist in our mind at the same time. The method of letting the negative thoughts pass is a powerful method.[1] In modern psychology, the process of replacing negative thoughts with positive ones is called 'cognitive reframing'.

Key words: Mind, Practice

1. Ricard Matthieu, Christophe Andre, and Alexandre Jollien, 2018. In Search of Wisdom: A Monk, a Philosopher, and a Psychiatrist on What Matters Most. Sounds True, Boulder, Colorado.

Negative thoughts, actions, and suffering

II.34 vitarka himsa adayah krta-karita-anumodita lobha-krodha-moha-purvaka mrdu-madhya-adhimatra duhkha-ajnana-ananta-phala iti pratipaksa-bhavanam

वि तर्क हिंसादय: कृत कारित अनुमोदिता लोभ क्रोध मोह पूर्वक मृदु मध्य अधिमात्रा दु:ख अज्ञान अनन्त फल इति प्रतिपक्ष भावनम् ।

vitarka: dubious knowledge, improper thoughts; himsa: violence, injuries; adayah: and so forth; krta: done; karita: done through others; anumodita: approved; lobha: greed; krodha: anger; moha: infatuation; purvaka: caused by; mrdu: mild; madhya: medium; adhimatra: and intense;

duhkha: pain; ajnana: ignorance; ananta: endless; phala: result; iti: thus; pratipaksa: opposite; bhavanam: feeling

Negative thoughts resulting from greed, anger and desire, injure and hurt others. These arise from ignorance about the actual, and ultimately bring pain and suffering. Even condoning or encouraging injurious and hurtful behaviors by others brings the same results. Focus on positive thoughts provides a counter current against negative thoughts and feelings.

This Sutra is a good example of a condensed message, typical of the Sutra tradition. It covers various aspects of thoughts and behaviors that cause suffering in life including how to reduce that suffering. It points out that actions that arise out of negative thoughts such as anger, greed or delusion have the potential to cause infinite misery and enhance ignorance. Dubious knowledge, directly or indirectly, gives rise to actions that bring violence, furthers falsehoods, and causes injustice. Whether such behaviors are approved, condoned, or are due to greed or anger or delusion, they cause suffering. Extreme acquisitiveness ultimately brings suffering to the greedy, injury to the procurers and providers of objects, and results in exploitation of the weak.

The reasons for suffering are usually in our behaviors. Sometimes there may not be any obvious causes. But ultimately, the root of all these is ignorance about reality, egocentricity, plus blindly following unexamined norms. It does not matter whether one overindulgences in pleasures, hurts others as well as oneself, incorporates others, or even approves them; they take one in the wrong direction. Focus on positive thoughts and corrective actions provide a counter current against negative thoughts and feelings.

Pain and suffering end through introspection. Introspection focused on all such aspects of experiences helps, in understanding the causes of and weighing in of proper responses, and for relieving pain and distress. Anger can be tamed by calming options, such as, intolerance by kindness and desire through practicing contentment. Use of the discriminating faculty helps one approach and handle the negative feelings that arise.

Key words: Afflictions, Mind, Practice

Positive effects of practicing non-violence

II.35   ahimsa pratisthayam tat-samnidhau vaira-tyagah

अहिंसा प्रतिष्ठायाम् तत् संन्निधौ वैर त्याग: ।

ahimsa: non-violence; pratisthayam: being grounded in;

tat-samnidhau: in her vicinity; vaira: hostility; tyagah: abandonment

When the practitioner is well-grounded in non-violence there is no hostility in her presence.

Making appropriate choices matters. Peaceful thoughts, words and actions create goodwill and that induces others to abandon hostility and cultivate friendly attitudes. Peace is contagious and transforms those who encounter a person at ease with herself and in her surroundings. It makes others feel peaceful too. While peace is conducive for nurturing harmony, violence is the weapon of disharmony. Because all beings are aware, the principle of non-harming applies to them too. Using them for our own purposes without any regard for their suffering is unacceptable.

There is the well-known story of two birds on a tree. One is frantically tasting all the fruit that is available, whereas, the other who has had its share, is quietly and peacefully sitting observing the other. Eventually the frantic bird calms down and sits quietly on the tree. Its mental energy, in the form of agitated feelings, is drawn towards the peaceful state of the other, thus producing a calming effect.

Key words: Ethics, Practice

Truth in actions

II.36 satya pratisthayam kriya phala asrayatvam

सत्य प्रतिष्ठायाम् क्रिया फल आश्रयात्वम् ।

satya: truth; pratisthayam: on being firmly established,
kriya: action; phala: fruit; asrayatvam: foundation

Adherence to truth depends on actions.

Intentions and actions are powerful. Words have power to do harm and to heal. Intention and willpower matter in exercising truthfulness. By adhering whole heartedly to the path of truth one has the power to create the desired reality. Then others are also energized to follow the path to truth. When attention is paid to expressed, and unexpressed thoughts and feelings, one is less likely to hurt the other. Nothing is as convincing as truth.

The Mundaka Upanishad (3.I.6) says: सत्यमेव जयते

Satyameva jayate (It is truth that conquers)

Key words: Attention, Ethics

Non-covetousness is rewarding

II.37 asteya pratisthayam sarva ratna upasthanam

अस्तेय प्रतिष्ठायाम् सर्व रत्न उपस्थानम् ।

asteya: non-stealing; pratisthayam: on being firmly

established; sarva: all; ratna: gems; upasthanam: coming

up

All riches become available to one who is firmly established in honesty.

An attitude of indifference to precious things, not coveting what others have, opens the doors to those very precious things and they become available to a greed-free person. This is because others trust an honest person and they feel confident and free to share what they have of value. The available gems referred to in the Sutra is a metaphorical expression and is to be interpreted as things that are truly meaningful and deeply satisfying in life, values such as love, peace, and sound relationships.

Key words: Afflictions, Ethics

Self-control energizes

II.38 brahmacharya pratisthayam virya labhah

ब्रह्मचर्य प्रतिष्ठायाम् वीर्य लाभ: ।

brahmacharya: self-restraint; pratisthayam: on being firmly

established; virya: vigor; labhah: gain

Vigor comes to one who masters self-control.

Cultivating a strong will-power is an important part of the yogic discipline. Brahmacharya literally means celibacy, but it may be interpreted as moderation, appropriate containment and channeling of life energy. The brain is a major user of energy. Therefore, the containment of life energy suggested here applies to all active areas of our life, physical, mental and intellectual.

In today's world, there are multiple choices available to us and pursuing those many times becomes draining and futile. Sometimes we make a choice by habit, automatically, and without giving it much consideration. Making a deliberate choice takes time and effort, plus there are always distractions. It takes self-control and weighing of options.

Inadequate containment and lack of direction dissipates energy, making it unavailable for attaining the objective in any endeavor. Thoughts and desires can be draining. Meditative techniques and practicing containment help calm the mind.

Key words: Ethics, Practice

<u>Detachment helps search for meaningfulness</u>

II.39 aparigraha-sthairye janma-kathamta-sambodhah

अपरिग्रह स्थैर्ये जन्म कथंता संबोध: ।

aparigraha: non-possessiveness; sthairye: on becoming steady; janma: birth; kathamta: the 'how; and 'wherefore'; sambodhah: knowledge

Greedlessness gives knowledge of the nature and purpose of existence.

Graha means to grasp and pari means things. Aparigraha means not grasping things. This Sutra points out that when one can remain immune to the pull of cravings, and there is detachment towards material possessions, one becomes aware of the bigger bounties of life. Holding on to experiences and beliefs is confining and leads to rigid patterns of thoughts and behaviors. Living a life free of conditioning, unencumbered by possessions and free of greed simplifies it.

A satisfied mind is free of wavering thoughts and desires, and there is enhanced self-understanding. It nurtures patience and interest in non-material matters. When one dwells on the true meaning of experiences, of life and of relationships, one under-stands the difference between what is meaningful and what is meaningless in life.

Key words: Ethics

Purity for distancing from the unhealthy

II.40　saucat sva-anga-jugupsa parair asamsargah

शौचात् स्वांग जुगुप्सा परैर असंसर्ग: ।

saucat: from purity; svanga: body; jugupsa: disgust; parair: with others; asamsargah: non-contact

Dis-identify with the body and ensure purity in contact with others.

What is a pure body? It is a body that is in balance, physio-logically and at ease with others. The Sanskrit word, 'jugupsa' in the Sutra, is translated as disgust by some commentators. There-fore, according to them, this emphasis on purity means develop-ing a dislike, an aversion, for the body, one's own as well as that of others. This puritanical sounding interpretation may have been consistent with the intense focus on spirituality in old times, when that really meant detachment from all things material, including the body. On the other hand, one of the earlier meanings of the word 'jugupsa' is concealment of what is undesirable, that which suggests protection. The body needs protection from anything that is harmful, toxic, unappealing, and stressful. Distancing oneself from such things is part of that. As for shunning contact with others, the suggestion is for seeking solitude, which is conducive for contemplation. It also suggests disinterest in cultivating relationships in an inappropriate way for enhancing one's own ego.

In modern times, there is the focus on attaining an exquisite body. Working at sculpting a beautiful body shape becomes an important part of self-image. But an undue, unhealthy focus on the appearance of the body is something that is counter-productive to seeking peace. When attention is focused on something as superficial and impermanent as the body, one forgets that the body is a valuable vehicle for self-realization and, also for understanding the feelings and emotions of others. A detached attitude with a healthy respect for the body and its important role in attaining refined understanding of other minds is more helpful. The body is the instrument of enlightenment, and a balance should be found between denial and contempt, on the one hand, and obsession with the body on the other. Purifying conditioned ways of looking at everything is part of distancing from the superficial and instead focusing on the subtle. Given the stressful ways of modern living, maintaining a peaceful and calm mind in a healthy body is a more appropriate focus.

Key words: Mind, Practice, Self

Purity of mind

II.41 sattva shuddhi saumansya eka agrya indriya jaya atma-
darshana-yogyatvani ca

सत्व शुध्दि सौमनस्य ऐकाग्र्य इन्द्रिय जय आत्म दर्शन योग्यत्वानि च ।

sattva shuddhi: purity of senses; saumansya: cheerful ness; ekagrya: one-pointedness; indriya jaya: mastery of senses; atma-darshana: vision of the soul; yogyatvani: fitness for; ca: and

Mental purity brings about cheerfulness, one-pointedness, mastery over the senses and the ability to understand oneself.

Memories always demand attention. Attending to those is like holding on to something while life is flowing by. Since memories do not stay silent, they can be burdensome. Certain memories are needed and are worth keeping. But one needs to let go of some old, sticky, and painful memories; so that there is room for better new ones. This keeps the mind ready for renewal and for maintaining freshness.

A mind that is free of cumbersome memories is pure and uncluttered. In such a mind the illuminative, wisdom oriented peaceful energies are activated through practicing self-disciplines (see Sutra II.32). Desires and attachments weaken. A pride-free mind is cheerful and the senses do not interfere while one tries to concentrate. Reactivity is diminished and there is no resistance to moving in the desired direction. A balanced mind represents a higher form of intelligence that helps understand one's real identity and the world around.

Key words: Mind, Practice

The rewards of contentment

II.42 samtoshad annuttamah sukha labhah

संतोषाद् अनुत्तम: सुख लाभ: ।

samtosad: from contentment; annuttamah: unexcelled;
sukha: happiness; labhah: gain

Contentment brings superlative happiness.

While the thirst for life pulls us outwards, satisfying desires does not bring as much happiness as contentment does. Satisfaction never lasts and desires soon reemerge. Contentment helps turn attention inwards, and one feels fulfilled. Cravings are replaced by the secure feeling that nothing is lacking. The energy released can be directed towards savoring the blissful state of a mind free of the pull of mundane desires.

Key words: Afflictions, Practice

<u>Strong commitment strengthens body and mind</u>

II.43 kayendriya-siddhih-asuddhi-ksayat-tapasah

काय इन्द्रिय सिद्धि: अशुद्धि क्षयात् तपस: ।

kaya: body; indriya: sense organs; siddhi: powers; asuddhi: impurity; ksayat: gradual destruction; tapasah: intense dedication

Austere life destroys impurities and the sense organs and the body are perfected.

This sutra is about the importance of dedicated commitment to the discipline. A strong resolve in following ethical norms (Sutra II.3) and practicing self-disciplines (Sutra II.32) gives mastery over the body and the senses, both being instrumental in the exploration of consciousness, the subject matter of the Yoga discipline. Following the appropriate self-set limits helps the body to endure the rigors of discipline and the senses are brought under control. These, further help clear any obstacles and distractions in the path.

Key words: Mind, Practice

Self-understanding

II.44 swadhyayad-ista-devata-samprayogah

स्वाध्यायाद इष्ट देवता संप्रयोग: ।

svadhyad: from self-study; ista-devata: desired deity; samprayogah: union

Self-study brings about union with the desired deity.

The study of the body, the senses, and reading scriptures usher in the calming experience. Meditative techniques, including recitation of mantras, also play an important role in that practice. A mantra means that which protects the mind, diverts it from holding on to thoughts that bring suffering and mental confusion. Devotion to a desired deity weakens the hold of ego and facilitates introspective understanding. One gains an understanding of the dynamics between our inner and outer realities.

Key words: Practice, Self

Surrender for total absorption

II.45 samadhi siddhih ishvar pranidhnat

समाधि सिद्धि: ईश्वर प्रणिधानात् ।

samadhi: absorption; siddhih: success; Ishvar: God; pranidhnat: by surrender

Surrender to God helps attain Samadhi

While concentration and meditation facilitate introspection, ultimately it is total devotion that helps in attaining the goal of Yoga. Surrendering to God, to a higher power, to a meaningful objective, is freeing and that helps in attaining the state of total absorption in any effort. That is Samadhi. In such a state the hold of ego, mundane attractions, pull of distractions, is weakened and the mind is at peace. This means that one can concentrate and fully focus on the object of concentration culminating in total immersion into the process of attaining that peace.

Key words: Practice, Self

Steady and comfortable posture

II.46 sthira sukham asanam

स्थिर सुखम् आसनम् ।

sthira: steady; sukham: comfortable; asanam: posture

Posture should be steady and comfortable.

When the Sutras appeared more than 2000 years ago, postures usually meant seated postures for meditation. In meditative postures, in addition to maintaining comfort, another major consideration is effortlessness in persevering. The body is one of the important reasons for our having disturbing thoughts. An uncomfortable or unhealthy body is not likely to be at ease with itself. Until the discomforts or pains are removed, one cannot concentrate. Any distraction from the body can thus, be problematic for maintaining an inward focus.

Asanas evolved and multiplied in the subsequent centuries. However, whatever form the body may take in any asana, in Patanjali's Yoga, asanas function as a meditative tool. Force and effort are selectively and judiciously applied. More importantly, an asana needs to have right alignment, and a stable and comfortable form. For maintaining an unobstructed flow of energies, mental postures and emotional states matter too. It is important that an asana helps direct awareness towards the deeper levels of consciousness within. A practitioner needs to be vigilant in attending to a steady and comfortable position. A healthy body and mind facilitate mastering a posture. And a steady posture is an important part of supporting a meditative attitude.

Key words: Practice, Self

Effortlessness in body and meditation

II.47   prayatna-saithilya-ananta-samapattibhyam

प्रयत्न शैथिल्य अनन्त समापत्तिभ्याम् ।

prayatna: effort; saithilya: relaxation; ananta: endless; samapatti: absorption by meditation

A posture is mastered by relaxing effort and keeping the mind absorbed in the infinite.

Patanjali recognizes the importance of the body in understanding the mind. Health of the body does not mean physical strength alone. We need endurance, stamina, flexibility, muscle coordination, stability, and ability to maintain balance. For that purpose, asanas become an important part of the discipline. In asana practice certain muscles that are not directly involved are kept in a relaxed condition. It brings about a sense of ease.

A posture is perfected when there is no effort, prayatna, needed to maintain it. One then reaches a relaxed state and sensitivity is extended to all parts of the body. When there is comfort, effortlessness, and muscles are relaxed, the body and the mind are in a receptive state. One is then easily drawn into a meditative state. With attention, perseverance and insight, the practitioner can stay immersed in a blissful state of harmony and complete absorption in the infinite space within and beyond.

Key words: Mind, Practice

Easing a conflicted mind

II.48 tato dvandva-anabhighatah

ततो द्वंद्व अनभिगात: ।

tato: from that; dvandva: pairs of opposites: anabhighatah: cessation of disturbance

Then, one is unaffected by the dualities of the opposites.

Life is dynamic and there are changes and contradictions arising frequently that we need to navigate around. Cold and hot, pleasant and unpleasant, moral and immoral, just and unjust, mental and physical, and many such choices always present themselves to us. They are distracting and the unsettled conditions result in feeling stressed. Postural practice is about familiarizing oneself with the embedded emotions and feelings. Like the mental opposites listed above, there are bodily opposites in the form of heat or cold sensations, and relaxed and tense muscles. The simultaneous extension and relaxation of muscles and balancing the active and receptive energies are part of holding a posture. Through postures such opposing sensations are eased and one stays open to the incoming experience.

Asana practice through sense direction helps in reining in our passions, and impulsive reactivity. Correct posture means the hold of the rash tendencies on mind is weakened and one can make choices that are more reasoned and less reactive. Through asana one attains bodily steadiness and the mind attains a state of equanimity. A calm mind signifies absence of conflict. A properly performed asana is where the effort is fine tuned to the state where it is neither too little nor too much. When that state is reached one can relax and turn attention inwards. The relaxation diffuses throughout the body and there is a feeling of blissfulness.

Key words: Mind, Practice

<u>Breathing</u>

II.49 tasmin-sati svasa-prasvasyor-gati-vicchedah pranayamah

तस्मिन् सति श्वास प्रश्वासयोर गति विच्छेद: प्राणायाम: ।

tasmin: on this; sati: having accomplished; svasa-prasvasyor: inhalation and exhalation; gati: movement; vicchedah: break; pranayamah: breath regulation

Following proficiency in asana is pranayama, which is regulation of breathing; of inhalation, exhalation and the pauses in between.

In this Sutra Patanjali says that, when proficiency in asana is accomplished, it prepares the body and rests the mind for undertaking, pranayama, or breath control. Pranayama consists of the regulation of the incoming and outgoing breaths. Prana is life energy and ayama is its regulation, extension, prolongation and control. When life energy, prana, is enhanced through regulation, it brings strength to the body and the mind.

Our normal breathing tends to be irregular and the objective is to make it rhythmic by attending to the flow of air in and out, and the pauses in between. Attending to inhaling, exhaling and the pauses thereafter, helps focus attention. Mindful breathing helps cultivate restraint. Stabilization of breath becalms the mind. It also helps concentration by keeping distractions at bay.

Key words: Mind, Practice

<u>Breathing techniques</u>

II.50 bahya-abhyantara-stambha-vrttir desakala samkhyabhih paridrastah dirgha-suksmah

बाह्य आभ्यन्तर स्तम्भ वृत्ति: देश काल संख्याभि: परिद्रुष्ट: दीर्घ सूक्ष्म: ।

bahya, abhyantara: external and internal; stambha vrttir: held; desa: place; kala: time; samkhyabhih: and number; paridrasto: regulated; dirgh: prolonged; suksmah: subtle

Breathing consists of external and internal movements of air with pauses in between; it is regulated by place, time, and number, and (becomes progressively) prolonged and subtle.

This Sutra describes three types of breathing techniques for the learner. Bahya, meaning external, means no flow of air after exhalation. Antara, or internal, means flow cessation after inhalation. And stambh, is the pause or holding of breath, after inhalation and after exhalation. In this state, the breathing is so deep and subtle that it appears like a prolonged breath retention. There is then no movement of thoughts.

The place, desa, referred to is the lung capacity of the practitioner. It can also be interpreted as the outward reach of the airflow from the nostrils, and, internally whatever part of the body is incorporated. Breath can also be directed towards specific parts of the body. The 'kala' or time is the duration of the breath and the number refers to its rhythm. These movements are subtle or drawn out depending on the length of practice. Extremely slow breathing is indicative of a very advanced state in practice when the mind is completely disengaged from mundane distractions. A sustained and steady practice done regularly for long periods nurtures a focused state of mind. The smoothness of breath is indicative of concentration.

Key words: Mind, Practice

Slow, imperceptible breathing

II.51 bahyabhyantara visayksepi caturthah

बाह्य अभ्यंतर विषय अक्षेपी चतुर्थ: ।

bahya: external; abhyantara: internal; visay: range;
aksepi: going beyond; caturthah: the fourth

The fourth type of pranayama goes beyond the sphere of in and outbreaths; and is when breathing becomes effortless and non-deliberate.

Normally there are three movements in pranayama; inhalation, exhalation and retention or the pauses that follow both these. There is a fourth type of movement that comes when breathing becomes quiet and subtle. It is for the adept. This state transcends the usual three types of movements, mentioned above. In this, the breathing is so slow that it gives the impression of complete stoppage. This state represents a very advanced stage of psychic and physical development. With intensely focused attention, life energy is circulated throughout the body. It is a deep meditative state in which the mind and consciousness are still. There are few subliminal impressions and one abides in a sense of total harmony.

Key words: Mind, Practice

Clarity and wisdom

II.52 tatah ksiyate prakas avaranam

तत: क्षीयते प्रकाश आवरणम् ।

tatah: from that; ksiyate: dissolves; prakas: light; avaranam: covering

From that the covering of light of the intellect is dissolved.

As one becomes proficient in pranayama, all conditioning and illusions disappear. It is like dissolving the covering of light. There is a better understanding of the mind and of how we react in any given situation. When ignorance is cleared, the hold of ego, passions and fears subsides. The authentic real Self comes to the forefront, and clarity in thoughts emerges. In the fourth state described in the previous Sutra, true knowledge shines through as wisdom is gained. Therefore, pranayama is called the higher vidya or discipline that provides the pathway to well-being, freedom and bliss.

Key words: Practice, Wisdom

Concentration

II.53 dharanasu cha yogyata manasah

धारणासु च योग्यता मनस: ।

dharanasu: for concentration; cha: and; yogyata: fit ness; manasah: of the mind

And it prepares the mind for concentration.

Pranayama, the intentional focus on inhalations and exhalations, quiets the mind which otherwise is subject to the pulls of the senses. Weakening such pulls gives the mind stability and prepares it for the next practice, that of concentration.

Key words: Attention, Mind, Practice

Redirecting attention from external to the internal

II.54 sva visaya asamprayoge chiita sva-rupa-aanukara iva indriyanam pratyaharah

स्व विषय असंप्रयोगे चित्त स्वरुप अनुकार इव इन्द्रियाणाम् प्रत्याहार: ।

sva: their own; visaya: objects; asamprayoge: disso ciation; chitta: individual mind; svarup: own form; anukara: following; iva: as if; indriyanam: by the sens es: pratyaharah: withdrawal

Pratyahara is the withdrawal of the senses from their objects.

The senses keep on drawing the mind towards the external world. On the other hand, when the mind is focused inwards, the senses cease to have any pull. The practice of pratyahara is intentionally reversing their pull and instead directing the mind in towards the self. The word 'pratyahara' means 'to draw towards the opposite'. By being selective and resisting the need for gratifying the senses, the mind can turn its attention inwards, towards the subconscious. Asana and pranayama are instrumental in preparing and cultivating such a change in perspective.

Key words: Attention, Mind, Practice

<u>Sense control for total attention</u>

II.55 tatah parama vasyata indriyanam

तत: परम वश्यता इन्द्रियाणाम् ।

tatah: from that; parama: the highest; vasyata: mas
tery; indriyanam: over the senses

Then follows the supreme mastery of the senses.

Pratyahara is the ability to withstand the pull of the senses. The senses serve the important function of connecting us to the world. They bring us joy as well as sorrow. Superficial and momentary pleasures draw attention away from focusing the mind on worth-while endeavors. We also like to protect ourselves against sensory pains that affect our ability to concentrate. For that it helps to cultivate the ability to resist the power of the senses. That ability is attained when the mind is becalmed because of practicing focusing attention on the body in asana and the breathing techniques. When the mind is free of distracting thoughts one can direct total attention wherever desired.

Key words: Attention, Mind, Practice

Chapter 5

III. Powers (Vibhuti)

In this chapter, meditation, mind, and the nature of the world are the three important subject areas. Patanjali cautions the practitioner about the powerful effects of the three-fold deep meditative discipline. They can be dangerous since they can give a false sense of mastery over self and others.

Sutras 1-3 are about the remaining three limbs in the Patanjali Ashtanga Yoga system, namely, the inner quest through concentration, meditation and total absorption.

<u>What is Concentration?</u>

III.1 desa-bandhah-cittasya dharana

देश बंध: चित्तस्य धारणा ।

desa: place; bandhah: fixing; cittasya: of the mind;

dharana: concentration

Concentration is confining attention within a limited field.

The practice of concentration is about training the mind for focusing attention. The mind tends to be drawn in various directions by multiple interests. Those are not simply distracting, they are also draining. To counter that, it helps to draw attention away from them and keep it focused on a sensation, thought, or activity. However, despite these options, the mind can still waver and flit back and forth between distractions. One needs practice to keep off interruptions in sustaining attention. Asana and pranayama, plus sense control practices, prepare the practitioner for concentration. Initially, attention wavers and needs to be drawn back to the subject of concentration, e.g., the body or the breath. Gradually, upon practice, it becomes easier to sustain it. Once some degree of ease in that is attained, gradually either the objects dissolve into the background or the diverse elements of the object of interest unfold. For example, it may be a sensation in the body, or an emotion; what it indicates, or what causes it.

Key words: Attention, Mind, Practice

What is Meditation?

III.2 tatra pratyaya-ekatanata dhyanam

तत्र प्रत्यय एकतानता ध्यानम् ।

tatra: there; pratyaya: device; ekatanata: continuous; dhyanam: meditation

Meditation is the uninterrupted flow of attention towards an object.

Meditation is the state when attention becomes continuous and steady, focused only on the object of concentration. Sense withdrawal and concentration precede and facilitate the meditative process. In meditation, there is no wavering of attention and therefore no resetting of focus. Instead it is a smooth flow of attention towards the gross and subtle aspects of the object, within its setting. When the focus is on a thought it can be viewed in an objective manner and that helps to free it of any conditioning.

Key words: Attention, Mind, Practice

<u>What is Samadhi?</u>

III.3 tadeva-artha- matra-nirbhasam svarupa-sunyam-iva samadhih

तदेव अर्थ मात्र निर् भासम् स्वरूप शून्यम् इव समाधि: ।

tadeva: the same; artha: the object; matra: only; nirb

hasam: shining; svarup: essential form; sunyam: empty;

iva: as if; samadhih: absorption

When the mind is totally absorbed in the object of meditation and nothing else, it is Samadhi.

Samadhi is the state of total absorption, wherein there is no separate awareness of the mind or of anything, apart from the object of focus. In this state, with the disappearance of the inter-vening thoughts, the form and essence of the object of focus is clearly reflected in the awareness within. One is totally absorbed in that awareness of the object only, while staying awake and alert. It is a very peaceful state and there are no extraneous thoughts intruding and demanding attention. Attention is total and completely free of subjectivity.

Key words: Attention, Practice

Sutras 4-8 focus on the meditative process, described as 'samyama' or deep meditation.

<u>What is deep meditation or 'Samyama'?</u>

III.4 trayam-ekatra samyamah

त्रयम् एकत्र संयम: ।

trayam: the three; ekatra: together; samyamah: concentration, meditation and absorption, all integrated.

Concentration, meditation and Samadhi together constitute Samyama.

The three practices referred to here, are concentration (Sutra III.1), meditation (Sutra III.2) and Samadhi or total absorption (Sutra III.3). The term 'Samyama', hereon referred to as deep meditation, represents the continuous process of attention with concentration, evolving into meditation, and subsequently attaining the state of total absorption, or Samadhi. Initially, after focusing attention on a single object, and keeping all distractions away, attention is sustained; and that is meditation. As that sustained attention continues one gets completely absorbed in the object of attention. Then all sense of separation between the meditator and the object dissolves and one becomes one with the object itself.

A novice practitioner may take some time to arrive at this level of proficiency, whereas an adept can arrive at the state of total absorption in a short time. It is characterized by dispassion and a progressive loosening of the hold of subjectivity. The transition from one state to another is continuous and smooth, resulting in a complete understanding of, and insight into the object of attention.

Key words: Attention, Practice

<u>The light of wisdom</u>

III.5   tat-jayat prajna-alokah

तज्जयात प्रज्ञा आलोक: ।

tat: that; jayat: mastery; prajna: wisdom; alokah: light

That gives the light of yogic insight or wisdom.

Upon mastering the technique of Samyama, the separation between the observer and the observed dissolves. There is a complete understanding of the nature of the objective world, including the mind, and its continuously changing nature. This state of discernment is wisdom. That enlightened worldview is liberating, and indicative of freedom from all suffering.

Key words: Mind, Reality, Wisdom

<u>Deep meditation practice</u>

III.6 tasya bhumisu viniyogah

तस्य भूमिषु विनियोग: ।

tasya: its; bhumisu: in stages; viniyogah: application

Its mastery is attained by stages.

In any venture or activity, the best results depend on the ability to hold attention. That ability can be cultivated, and is attainable through practice. Starting with concentration, and evolving through meditation, it takes varying lengths of time, to arrive at the state of complete absorption. It also depends on the practitioner herself, on her commitment to the process. Asana, pranayama, or meditation practice is effective when it suits individual temperament and needs. Since these practices are interdependent, one needs to get proficient in concentration before sustaining attention, and after that, one can attain the state of complete absorption. Besides, some objects of concentration, such as a candle, reveal their total nature quickly and something complex like the human psyche can take a long time to understand. In any case, the technique helps provide a complete understanding of anything that one chooses to.

Key words: Attention, Practice

<u>Internal practices</u>

III.7   trayam-antara-angam purvebhyah

त्रयम् अंतरंगम् पूर्वेभ्य: ।

trayam: trio; antar: inner; angam: limb, member;
purvebhyah: in relation to the preceding ones

These three practices are internal in relation to the preceding ones.

Among the eight limbs of Yoga, the first five are part of the preparatory stages in the Yogic discipline and relate to the external aspects of living and being. The five practices include, yama or ethical norms and are about actions in the societal setting; the niyama are about personal, physical, and mental disciplines; asana practice prepares the body; pranayama is about channeling the flow of life energy; and pratyahara is about sense perceptions. Together they help train the mind to maintain proper restraint and overcome impulsive/compulsive action. The ability to refrain from potentially hurtful actions is important for calming of mind and developing meditative focus.

The three practices that are part of 'the meditation discipline'; namely concentration (Dharana); meditation (Dhyana); and total absorption (Samadhi); constitute the inner limbs. These focus on the inner dimensions of living, meaning they are subjective and subtle. They represent the introspective process. They play an important role in the spiritual quest and prepare the ground for reaching even deeper levels of absorption.

Key words: Attention, Mind, Practice

Support-free meditation

III.8   tad-api bahir-angam nirbijasya

तत् अपि बहिर अंगम् निर्बिजस्य ।

tad: that; api: even; bahirangam: external parts; nirbijasya: seedless

The Sabija (with seed) Samadhi is external to the Nirbija (without seed) Samadhi.

The first five limbs of Yoga are based on the connection to the material world. The next three consist of concentration, meditation, plus complete absorption, or Samadhi. Initially, holding of attention is facilitated by focusing it on objects/thoughts. These are like seeds for the practice. Then, there is a deeper level of absorption that is seedless, that is, there is no need of an object or thought to anchor the attention. This represents a higher rung of the Yoga experience. The transcendence of the need for a seed is considered to be the ultimate level of the ability to meditate. At this stage, all conscious and subconscious impressions are held inactive. And compared to such seedless Samadhi, therefore, the one with seed remains external and connected with the world, Prakriti.

Key words: Attention, Practice, Reality

Sutras 9-12 are about calming of mind.

<u>Establishing silence between thoughts</u>

III.9 vyuthana-nirodha-samskaryor-abhibhava-pradur-bhavau
nirodha-kasna-cittaanavayo nirodha-parinamah

व्युत्थान निरोध संस्कारयोर अभिभव प्रादुर्भावौ निरोध क्षण चित्तान्वयो निरोध परिणाम: ।

vyuthana: outgoing; nirodha: restraint; samskaryor: of the impressions; abhibhava: disappearing; pradurbhavau: appearance; nirodhakasna: the unmodified state of mind; citta: mind; anavay: permeation; nirodha: restraint; parinamah: transformation

The momentary state between a disappearing impression and the incoming one is called Nirodha. And when it becomes established it is called Nirodha Parinama, meaning transformation towards silence.

When concentrating, there are momentary intervals when an impression is fading and another one has yet to arise. Mind wavers between attention and distraction. Individual behaviors, attitudes and expressions respond to the state that is dominant. When attention is to be sustained, the objective is to elongate moments of attention and shorten the moments of distraction. By learning to identify and focus attention on evolving phenomena and staying away from distraction, one can identify the silent gaps in between and learn to dwell on those. With practice, such silent moments become gradually stretched.

One of the Pranayama practices involves slowly elongating the pauses that follow inhalations and exhalations. This is helpful in extending silent moments. One learns to prevent incoming impressions from capturing the mind. Attending to such subtle movements in attention also helps in understanding the moment to moment changes in any sensation and experience.

Focusing and prolonging exhalations is another breathing technique that helps to hold off any new looming experience arising and capturing attention. In fact, the ability to restrain distracting influences on our minds is cultivated by following the 'do's and 'do nots' as prescribed in Yama and the Niyama. Asana practice too is helpful in being selective in how attention is directed towards specific parts of the body. The peaceful moments that ensue from these practices keep us drawn towards these practices instead of to the compulsive urges rising from the subconscious. This is the type of transformation that these practices bring about.

Key words: Attention, Mind, Practice

<u>Sustaining silent moments between thoughts</u>

III.10 tasya prashant-vahita samskarat

तस्य प्रशान्त वाहिता संस्कारात् ।

tasya: its; prashant: peaceful; vahita: flow; samskarat: by its (repeated) impression

Repeated impressions transform into a tranquil flow.

Regularly following these practices (mentioned above) helps in sustaining peaceful moments. The mind usually prefers to move away from the active to peaceful moments, and once experienced those become alluring. Repeated experiences of these strengthen these tendencies and weaken the push and pull of the old distracting experiences. This also prevents new diversionary ones from getting a foothold. Sustained practice is helpful in establishing such effectiveness.

Key words: Attention, Practice

Total absorption

III.11 sarvarthata ekagratayoh ksaya udayau cittasya samadhi parinamah

सर्वार्थता एकाग्रतयो: क्षय उदयौ चित्तस्य समाधि परिणाम: ।

sarvarthata: many pointedness; ekagratayoh: of one-pointedness; ksaya-udayau: decay and rise; cittasya: of the mind; Samadhi: absorption; parinamah: transformation

As one-pointedness is strengthened, distractions settle down and one attains the transformed state of total absorption.

The mind tends to be drawn simultaneously towards various things. The five senses take it to the past and to the future. Scattered attention usually results in superficiality, and feeling restless; whereas, one-pointed attention usually feels peaceful. When peaceful, the mind turns inwards. It becomes more receptive and open to subtle experiences pertaining to the object of attention. Any accomplishment, success in every area of interest, depends on such attention. When scattered attention is replaced by one-pointed attention, it brings about total absorption; and that is being in Samadhi.

Key words: Attention, Practice

<u>Sustained absorption into the object of attention</u>

III.12 tatah punah santa-uditau tulya-pratyayau chittasya-
ekagrata-parinamah

तत: पुन: शान्त उदितौ तुल्य प्रत्ययौ चित्तस्य एकाग्रता परिणाम: ।

tatah: then; punah: again; santa: subsided; uditau: risen;

tulya: equal; pratyayau: cognitions; cittasya: of the mind;

ekagrata: one-pointedness; parinamah: transformation

The state of the mind in which the object in the mind merges into an exactly similar object that follows in the next moment is called ekagrata parinama.

In the contemplative state attention is sustained and uninterrupted, mental activity and calm are balanced. The result of the ability to stay in contemplative silence is transformative. The mind stays away from intruding thoughts or bodily sensations. Such continuous flow of attention focused on an object is like an uninterrupted stream of identical pictures appearing one after another and that results in its image remaining unchanged in the mind's eye. Change makes us aware of the time. When the image of the object of concentration remains unchanged, it gives the illusion of time standing still.

Key word: Attention

Sutras III.13-16 are about the slow process of change. Here Patanjali's ideas precede the Darwinian Theory of Evolution.

<u>Understanding changes</u>

III.13 etena bhuta-indriyesu dharma-laksana-avastha-parinama vyakhyatah

एतेन भूत इन्द्रियेषु धर्म लक्षण अवस्था परिणाम व्याख्याता: ।

etena: by this; bhuta: in the elements; indriyesu: in the sense organs; dharma: property; laksana: character; avastha: condition; parinama: transformation; vyakhyatah: are explained

These (states of attention described in Sutras III. 10-12) explain the transformations of the mind and in the property, character, and condition of the elements and sense organs.

The preceding three types of attention states are transformative, in terms of our way of making sense of the world around and within us. Relieved of the hold of changing thoughts one gets an understanding of the changing nature of objects, including their inherent properties, forms, and states. This Sutra states that change is of three kinds, namely transforming in dharma (characteristics), laksana (time) and avastha (mode). Dharma-parinama means change caused by changes in characteristics, laksana parinama means change over time, and avastha parinama means change caused by mode. In fact, change (parinama) comes to be created by all three.

For example, there are certain inherent properties (dharma) of a substance such as wood; its appearance, texture, weight and feel etc. Then that substance may be transformed into a tool (mode), or paper. Here one realizes the cause and effect relationship behind such transformations. Either the paper or the tool can be in a new, worn or decayed form due to certain reasons, (time).

This applies to the body, mind and senses too. Our appearance, interests, and overall sense of the self evolves as time goes by. Everything changes and goes through these different types of transformations, changes in appearance or state, and qualities. While objects in Nature are acted upon by environmental forces, our bodies, senses and the mind respond to the environment and the choices we make.

In all these, objects or bodies, a range of interacting influences, sometimes slow, sometimes energizing, and sometimes opposing; are always operative. They bring about changes in the form, qualities and energies of anything material and non-material within and around us. In Nature materials have attributes (such as color, form), objects grow and decay. Similarly, our senses bring impressions that evolve into thoughts, memories, and these can be strong or weak.

A becalmed mind and focused mind is, therefore, instrumental in bringing to light the magnitude and nature of constantly evolving changes within and around us. A better understanding of reality, overt and subtle, helps develop the ability to make decisions that can enhance our ability to navigate through life.

Key words: Mind, Reality

<u>Unchanging foundation of everything</u>

III.14 santa-udita avyapadesya-dharma-anupati dharmi.

शान्त उदित अव्यपदेश्य धर्म अनुपाती धर्मी ।

santa: calm; udita: uprisen; avyapadesya: latent; dharma: property; anupati: follows; dharmi: where the property resides

The properties, latent, active, or un-manifest reside in an un-changing substratum.

The body and the mind change through time. Similarly, impressions of an experience, thought, or memory is always affected by time and, also, by other impressions, latent or active. Objects too, undergo transformations. An object, such as clay or water, consisting of certain basic elements, takes different forms. These forms change as time and conditions change. Yet that does not affect the original nature of its basic elements in clay. Similarly, the nature of the Self, the inborn awareness within us, the Purusha, the source of all our experiences, remains un-changed and unaffected.

Everything in the material world, the body/mind and objects that are part of Prakriti, is subject to the changing balance among the ever-present three energies, (the 'guna'), namely cognition, action, and retention, referred to previously in Sutras I.16, II.15, 19. The Yoga discipline enables the practitioner to understand all the changes that everything material undergoes. The past determines the form of the original material in the present, whereas, the present determines the future.

Key word: Reality

The process of change

III.15 krama-anyatvam parinama-anyatve hetuh

क्रम अन्यत्वं परिणाम अन्यत्वे हेतु: ।

krama: succession; anyatvam: variety; parinama:
transformation; anyatve: difference; hetuh: cause

The diversity of forms is due to the difference in the underlying process.

An object undergoes a certain sequential change and it attains a certain shape. A seed gets transformed into a tree upon going through a developmental process. For any change to happen the appropriate conditions must be present. In Nature and, in our body/mind, changes are taking place all the time and at different rates in all the constituent entities. Only after some time they manifest as tangible transformations. Our mind and overall consciousness, like objects, undergo changes through time, and any altered identifiable character in those may manifest later. Appropriate environmental conditions as well as individual effort, aptitudes and skills matter. Success in Yoga depends on mastering the prescribed techniques. Until one learns to keep off diversions, concentration and full absorption are difficult to achieve, and when achieved the effects may appear incrementally, and over time.

An adept practitioner is eventually able to identify and understand the progression of changes in her past and present, and how they are likely to evolve. The process of change in both objective, and subjective realities manifests in concrete, identifiable form, eventually.

Key words: Practice, Reality

Knowing subjective and objective realities
III.16 parinama-traya samyamat atita anagata jnanam

परिणाम त्रय संयमात् अतीत अनागत ज्ञानम् ।

parinama: transformations; traya: the three; samyamat: by deep meditation on; atita: past; anagata: future; jnanam: knowledge

By holding attention on the three types of transformations one gains knowledge of the past and the future.

When attention is focused, as in concentration, meditation and total absorption, it results in the three types of transformations described in the earlier Sutras (11-15). This means complete understanding of the properties, character and condition of objects and of the mind. Objects and senses help demonstrate the ever-changing nature of objective reality, as well as the nature of our psyche, our interactions with reality and with other beings. With self-experience and the mind as the tool of investigation, this provides an understanding of the past, present and possible future states and forms of everything.

Key words: Attention, Mind, Reality

A better understanding of reality can lead to acquiring certain powers and these are listed in the Sutras 17-48.

Communication and perception

III.17 sabda-artha-pratyayanam-itaretara-adhyasat-samkara-tat-pravibhaga-samyamat-sarva-bhuta-ruta-jnanam

शब्द अर्थ प्रत्ययानाम् इतरेतर अध्यासात् संकर तत् प्रविभाग संयमात् सर्व भूत रुत ज्ञानम् ।

sabda: word; artha: purpose; pratyayanam: feelings;
itaretara: one another; adhyasat: superimposing;
samkaras: mixture; tat: of them; pravibhaga: differentiation;
samyamat: by deep meditation on; sarva: all; bhuta: living
beings; ruta: sounds; jnanam: knowledge

It is confusing when the sound, its meaning, and its idea are present together. By concentrating on the sound, the confusion is resolved and one comprehends the meaning of sounds uttered by any living being.

This Sutra is about verbal communication. Words are commonly used to represent objects and convey thoughts. The listener assigns meaning to certain combinations of letters, and perception occurs. However, representation, meaning and perception are not the same. Representation and meaning are based on convention. But depending of the speaker's intention, differences in how words are used can present a different picture. Similarly, perception depends on the listener, her memories, emotional states and biases. Yogic skills of meditative absorption provide deep insights into the distinctions within all such aspects of communication. Some commentators claim that these skills also help in understanding other languages and cultures, as well as other species. One can say that this Sutra is about how the discipline of concentration enhances one's ability to decipher varied ways of communication, verbal and non-verbal, and understanding of the associated mental processes.

Key words: Mind, Practice

<u>Perceptions and behaviors</u>

III.18 samskar-saksat-karanat-purva-jati-jnanam

संस्कार साक्षात् करणात् पूर्व जाति ज्ञानम् ।

samskar: impressions; saksat: by observation; karanat: by making; purva: previous; jati: births; jnanam: knowledge

Knowledge of the previous births is gained through direct perception of the impressions.

This Sutra is about examining one's own impressions and tendencies that condition us to opting for certain types of actions. Impressions and perceptions leave their imprints on our minds. Concentrating on these provides understanding of the past but also of previous life experiences. Therefore, by following the deep meditation discipline (concentration, meditation and total absorption), a proficient practitioner attains the ability to reach into the deepest and farthest parts of consciousness that hold impressions from not only current but also from previous life-experiences and their consequent manifestations as predispositions towards specific forms of behavior and thinking. This enhances self-knowledge.

Key words: Attention, Mind, Practice

<u>Empathy</u>

III.19 pratyayasya para-citta-jnanam

प्रत्ययस्य पर चित्त ज्ञानम् ।

pratyayasya: perception; para: other; citta: mind; jnanam: knowledge

Through direct perception one gets knowledge of the minds of others.

This Sutra is about understanding others. It suggests that when the practitioner attains complete understanding of her own mind, she can also then, read the minds of others. The connection with others is strengthened. She can put her own thoughts aside and there is acuity in her perceptive abilities resulting from the meditative discipline.

Abraham Lincoln said that we are responsible for the face we present to others. Our thoughts and actions leave their imprints on us. Appearance, demeanor, and body language provide important clues about others and nurture certain instinctive reactions, and subtle impressions of others in our minds. By concentrating on our experiences with others we gain an understanding of their minds too. There is increased empathy when we can shift attention totally towards them. The deep meditation discipline is instrumental in strengthening this ability to read other minds.

Key words: Attention, Mind, Practice

<u>Knowing other minds, not the objects thereof.</u>

III.20 na ca tat sa-alambanam tasya-avisayi-bhutavat

न च तत् सालंबनं तस्य अविषयी भूतत्वात् ।

na: not; ca: and; tat: that; sa: with; alambanam: with support; tasya: that; avisayi: beyond the reach pf mind; bhutavat: in this life

With the deep meditation discipline one knows the general quality of other minds, but not what their thoughts are about.

This Sutra informs that an accomplished Yogi's knowledge is limited when it comes to the minds of others. An adept practitioner can read someone else's emotional states and thoughts but does not necessarily have any information about what may be the object of the thoughts in those minds. The reason being those objects are not part of the meditative focus, the overall mind state is.

Key words: Mind

<u>Invisibility</u>

III.21 kaya rupa samyamat tad grahya sakti stambhe caksuh prakasa asamprayoge antardhanam

कायरूप संयमात् तद्ग्राह्य शक्ति स्तंभे चक्षु: प्रकाश असंप्रयोगे अन्तर्धानम् ।

kaya: body; rupa: form; samyamat: deep meditation; tad: from it; grahya: receptive; sakti: power; stambhe: on suspension; caksuh: eye; prakasa: light; asamprayoge: disconnection; antardhanam: disappearance

Deep meditation makes the body invisible as the contact between the observer's eye and light from the body is broken.

Among the supposed accomplishments of an adept is the ability to become invisible at will. How does the Yogi become invisible? The observation that when the contact between the observer's eye and the light from the body is severed, the Yogi becomes invisible; is unclear. Perhaps, there is another interpretation. This may refer to the practitioner merging so well into the background as to be unnoticeable. One who has conquered ego lets the accomplishments of others shine and she herself remains almost unperceived, merging into the background.

Key words: Practice, Self

<u>Actions</u>

III.22 sopakramam nirupkramam ca karma tat-samyamat
aparanta-jnanam aristebhyah va

सोपक्रमम् निरुप क्रमम् च कर्म तत् संयमात् अपरान्त ज्ञानम् अरिष्टेभ्य:
वा ।

sopakramam: immediate effect; nirupkramam: dormant;
ca: and; karma: actions; tat: them; samyamat: by deep
meditation on; aparanta: death; jnanam: knowledge;
aristebhyah: from omens; va: or

Karma is of two kinds: active and dormant. With deep meditation
focused on karma, one gets understanding of omens or forewarn-
ing of death.

Actions have effects; some effects manifest immediately
and some later. For every action there are two kinds of effects;
those that have an impact on other beings and things, and those
that affect the subject of the action, the doer. The former effects
are inevitable, the latter kind are not. Normally actions affect the
doers too. But when there is no attachment behind an action, and
it is undertaken for the good of others, it does not affect the doer.
Through deep meditation on actions one can understand all such
effects, one's present, and what is to be expected in the future.
That gives an opportunity to correct and redirect our efforts in the
right direction. There are, sometimes, omens and signs that are
suggestive of the likely happenings. An adept meditator can not
only sense those but also decipher what they suggest.

Key words: Attention, Practice

Strength in sharing

III.23 maitry-adishu balani

मैत्रिय आदिषु बलानि ।

maitry: friendliness; adishu: so forth; balani: of powers

By meditation on friendliness and other virtues, moral and emotional strengths are acquired.

Sutra I.33 prescribes cultivating certain virtues; namely friendliness, compassion, joyousness and equanimity. This Sutra says that friendly attitudes draw people together and thereby strengthen all. The feeling of separation from others is weakened. Feeling compassion for those who are struggling, brings in the desire to pull them out of their suffering. This also has the effect of distancing oneself from one's own problems. Sharing joy with others is uplifting. This Sutra says that by meditating on such attributes the practitioner gains moral and emotional strength and can keep away anger, envy, and pride.

Key words: Practice, Self, Wisdom

Strength follows determination

III.24 baleshu hasti-baladini

बलेषु हस्ति बलादीनि ।

baleshu: (deep meditation) on strength; hasti: elephant; bala: strength; adini: of others

By concentrating on strength, the yogi gains the strength of elephants.

By practicing deep meditation on strength, physical or mental, the practitioner can gain the strength of an elephant or a warrior. A focused and determined mind can overcome any obstacle and is empowering in any venture. That focus is conducive to actualizing all different strengths within us.

Key words: Attention, Practice

Sustained attention draws everything close

III.25 pravrtti-aloka-nyasat suksma-vyavahita-viprakrsta-jnanam

प्रवृत्ति आलोक न्यासात् सूक्ष्म व्यवहित विप्रकृष्ट ज्ञानम् ।

pravrtti: cognitive faculties; aloka: light; nyasat: by directing; suksma: of the small; vyavahita: hidden; viprakrsta: distant; jnanam: knowledge

One gains knowledge of small things, hidden or distant, by directing the light of illuminating cognition.

The qualities of sustained and keen observation cultivated through the deep meditative discipline can shed light on the subtlest forms of nature anywhere. With such super-perceptive faculties, the practitioner gains knowledge of things small and large, near and distant, and in sight or beyond sight.

Key words: Attention, Practice

Sustained attention for knowledge

III.26 bhuvana-jnanam surye samyamat

भूवन ज्ञानं सूर्ये संयमात् ।

bhuvana: of the worlds; jnanam: knowledge; surye: on the sun; samyamat: by deep meditation on

By deep meditation on the sun one gets knowledge of the seven worlds.

This and the next two Sutras say that meditation on the sun, the moon and the Pole star yields knowledge about the whole celestial system, the solar system, and the positions and movements of stars. These Sutras may also be metaphorical; with the sun, moon and the Pole star representing different areas of the cosmos or parts of the body and their associated functional roles. For example, the sun represents energy. Thus, by making the sun the focus of meditation, the practitioner gains an understanding of the solar plexus, located in the trunk of the body. This part of the body, according to the Ayurvedic chakra concept, is about reasoning abilities, questioning, research and formulating explanations. (More about chakras follows soon.) Understanding this part of body, therefore, yields knowledge of everything in the body.

Key words: Attention, Practice

<u>Calming energy</u>

III.27 candre tara-vyuha jnanam

चंद्रे तारा व्यूह ज्ञानम् ।

candre: (deep meditation) on the moon; tara: of star; vyuha: organization; jnanam: knowledge

Meditation on the moon gives knowledge about the arrangement of stars.

This Sutra, like the previous ones, is about the power of focused attention. Therefore, when the moon, is the focus of meditation, one gains information about the position of stars.

Metaphorically speaking, the lunar (feminine, yin) energy channel of the body is represented by the Ida Nadi, on the left side of the spine. Nadi means flow, and the moon represents serenity. The Ida Nadi controls mental processes, and by fostering devotional, caring tendencies, it facilitates the flow of consciousness towards the divine. This has a calming effect on the mind.

Key words: Attention, Mind, Practice

Rewards of immovable attention

III.28 dhruve tad-gati-jnanam

ध्रुवे तद् गति ज्ञानम् ।

dhruve: (deep meditation on) the pole star; tad: its; gati: movement; jnanam: knowledge

Meditation on the pole-star gives knowledge of movement of stars.

The Pole star, which maintains a fixed position in the sky, is about steadfastness. It helps identify the motion of other stars. Metaphorically speaking this may be interpreted as focusing attention on anything that provides stability; for example, parents, or revered teachers. Such focus helps understand the movements within any system, the body or the society.

Key words: Practice

Sutras III.29-34 are about meditating on specific part of the body.

Importance of the navel area of the body

III.29 nabhi-cakre kaya-vyuha-jnanam

नाभि चक्रे काय व्यूह ज्ञानम् ।

nabhi-cakre: (deep meditation on) the navel energy center; kaya: body; vyuha: organization: jnanam: knowledge

Meditation on the navel yields knowledge about the body system.

Meditation focused on the navel provides understanding of the working of the navel area that plays an important part in breathing and therefore in the circulation of life energy or prana. This sutra refers to the chakra concept. In yoga philosophy, like the physical and mental body, we have an energy body which is the network of chakras and energy pathways, or nadis. A Chakra is a non-physical center of energy. There are seven such energy centers located in different parts of the body. Each chakra receives, takes in and expresses prana, the life energy force. The nabhi-chakra, the third one located at the navel, is about body energy as well as about identity. Self-esteem, digestion, metabolism, aggressive energy, are all associated with this chakra. Supposedly, the nadis, or energy channels, are centered in the navel area and branch out from there throughout the body. Therefore, the meditative discipline focused on this area of the body provides important insights into the health of different parts of body.

Key words: Mind, Practice

Expression and feeling secure

III.30 kantha-kupe ksut-pipasa-nivrttih

कंठ कूपे क्षुत् पिपासा निवृत्ति: ।

kantha: throat; kupe: well; ksut: of hunger; pipasa: thirst; nivrttih: cessation

There is no hunger or thirst when one meditates on the throat.

Deep meditation centered on any part of the body ushers in calm and tranquil states of mind. The throat is about expression and creativity. And the throat (Vishuddhi) chakra, is the focus of verbalization, singing and creativity. We create our world through words, and the sounds we make. Self-expression is the domain of this chakra. Absence of hunger or thirst can be interpreted as being indicative of feeling secure and accepted.

Key words: Mind, Practice

<u>Deep-seated mind energies</u>

III.31 kurma nadyam sthairyam

कूर्म नाड्यम् स्थैर्यम् ।

kurma: tortoise; nadyam: nerve; sthairyam: steadiness

The mind and body become firm and steady when one meditates on the kurma nadi

Kurma nadi channels and regulates emotional energy. Kurma is tortoise. Below the trachea is the tubular structure that is shaped like a tortoise. Nadis are the energy channels that convey energy from the energy centers throughout the body. In this case when, in deep meditation, attention is focused on the tortoise or Kurma energy channel, the mind and body take on the characteristics of the tortoise, namely, its firmness and steadiness. There are instinctive energies hidden in the unconscious. The tortoise represents such energies ruling the subconscious mind. Like a tortoise pulling its limbs under; in meditation, attention is drawn inwards and restlessness is brought under control. This strengthens the body and emotional stability is attained.

Key words: Mind, Practice

Connecting with the enlightened

III.32 murdha-jyotisi siddha-darsanam

मूर्ध ज्योतिषि सिद्ध दर्शनम् ।

murdha: the head; murdha-jyotisi: light under the skull; siddha: perfected beings; darsanam: vision of

Meditation on the light under the crown of the head brings vision of perfected beings.

The crown chakra at the top of the head is called the sahasrara chakra. This is the seat of the most evolved consciousness. When one meditates on the crown of the head, one gets visions of accomplished Yogis. Such persons provide guidance and inspiration and one gets a better understanding of oneself, of others, and of everything else.

Key words: Mind, Practice

Power of intuition

II.33 pratibhat va sarvam

प्रतिभात् वा सर्वम् ।

pratibhat: from intuitive knowledge; va: or; sarvam: everything

Or by intuition, comes (knowledge of) everything.

Perceptive abilities are strengthened through dedicated practice. The realization that everything fits together appears when the perfected state is reached. One does not need sensory input for arriving at the understanding of anything and knowledge appears as a flash of lightening. An accomplished Yogi can intuit everything and attains discriminative knowledge.

Key words: Wisdom

The mind and emotions

III.34 hrdaye citta-samvit

हृदये चित्त संवित् ।

hrday: heart; hrdaye: on the heart; citta-samvit:

awareness of the mind

Meditation centered on the heart brings awareness of the nature of the mind.

There is the long-held belief that the heart is the center of intelligence and the place where consciousness resides. It is the center of perception and insight, nurturance and of feelings and emotions. Meditation centered on the heart (Anahata) chakra therefore yields knowledge of the mind. A strong anahata chakra is associated with deep understanding of human nature, a toler-ant and helpful attitude towards resolving conflicts.

Key words: Mind, Practice

World experience vs. awareness

III.35 sattva-purusayoh atyanta asamkirnayoh pratyaya aviseso bhogah parathatvat svartha-samyamat purusa-jnanam

सत्व पुरुषयो: अत्यन्त असंकीर्णयो: प्रत्यय अविशेषो भोग: परार्थत्वात स्वार्थ संयमात पुरुष ज्ञानम् ।

sattva-purusayor: represents refined intellect; atyanta: extremely; asamkirnayoh: distinctive; pratyaya: of awareness; aviseso: non-distinct; bhogah: experience; parathatvat: apart from other's interest: svartha: self-interest; samyamat: deep meditation on Self; purusa-jnanam: knowledge of Self.

In the worldly experience, we are unable to distinguish between our Self and Sattva, or the serene state of mind. These two are completely distinct. The purpose of worldly experience is for serving the Self or Purusha.

Buddhi or intelligence, like the rest of the mind, is part of Nature (Prakriti) and therefore totally different from the Self, the knower within (Purusha). Intelligence delivers world experience to the knower. When the intelligence is free of self-centeredness, it has the qualities of balance and serenity ('sattva') and active ('rajas') and resistant energies ('tamas' 'guna') stay latent. The serene, pleasant and blissful experiences associated with such intelligence, are not those of the knower herself, but reflections of the knower. Meditating on the balanced and serene intelligence gives us an understanding of Self through direct self-experience.

Key words: Mind, Practice, Self

A strong mind

III.36 tatah pratibha-sravana-vedana adarsa asvada-varta jayante

तत: प्रतिभ श्रवण चेदनादर्श स्वाद वार्ता जायंते ।

tatah: thence; pratibha: intuitional; sravana: auditory;
vedana: tactile; adarsa: visual; asvada: taste; varta: smell;
jayante: are born

From this, intuition as well as knowledge of super hearing, touch, vision, taste, and smell are born.

When the attention is focused on understanding the nature of the knower, the intuitive quality of Self, that all beings possess, is enhanced. The senses become free and their acuity strengthens. This helps in gaining a better understanding of everything experienced and facilitates self-discovery.

Key words: Mind, Practice, Self, Wisdom

<u>Powers distract</u>

III.37 te samadhou upsargah vyutthane siddhayah

ते समाधौ उपसर्ग व्युत्थाने सिद्धय: ।

te: they; samadhou: in Samadhi; upsarga: obstacles;
vyutthane: outward oriented; siddhayah: powers

When the mind is outward oriented, it becomes an obstacle to attaining absorption (Samadhi).

The various above-mentioned special powers that result from following the meditation discipline can come in the way of attaining Samadhi, the ultimate state of meditative absorption. They create attachments and strengthen the hold of ego. Samadhi depends on the mind turning inwards and away from the external world. The special powers are therefore distracting, as they pull the mind towards worldly experiences. These inevitably bring on apprehensions and fears. The objective is to see and experience the material world (Prakriti) in an unconditioned way, described as pure seeing, that is arrived at only when one can attain the state of deep absorption.

Key words: Mind, Practice

<u>Understanding the body and the mind</u>

III.38 bandha-karana-saithilyat pracara-samvednac ca cittasya para-sariravesah

बन्ध कारण शैथिल्यात् प्रचार संवेदनात् च चित्तस्य पर शरीर आवेश: ।

bandha: bondage; karana: cause; saithilyat: relaxation; pracara: flow: samvednac: from knowledge of; ca: and; cittasya: of the mind; para: another; sarira: body; avesah: entrance

Free of the bondage of body and with knowledge of the mind the yogi can know another mind at will.

The body is tied to the senses, thoughts and actions. Self-understanding frees the mind from the hold of repeated actions and the impressions they leave on the body. The accomplished Yogi, as a result, can dissociate herself from the body. This helps in understanding the minds and actions of others as well, the obvious as well as the deeper dimensions of their thought processes. However, such enhanced understanding of others can feed the ego. This can have a distracting effect on the practitioner. It takes an accomplished Yogi to understand and undo the hold of ego.

Key words: Afflictions, Mind, Practice

Upward moving energy

III.39 udana-jayat jala panka-kantak adisu asangah utkrantih ca

उदान जयात् जल पंक कंण्टक आदिशु असंग उत्क्रांति च ।

udana: upward moving air; jayat: by mastery; jala: water; panka: mire; kantaka: thorns; adisu: the rest; asanga: non-contact; utkrantih: levitation; ca: and

By mastering upward rising life breath one can rise above water, mire and thorns.

Udana, one of the five forms of the life energy, moves upwards from the lungs, against the gravitational pull. It controls the vocal chords, regulates cognitive skills and memory, and intake of air and food. It is active between the heart and the brain and delivers energy to the brain. It sustains body tissues. This energy, supposedly, makes the body feel light and the mind free. Sometimes this Sutra is interpreted as the power of overcoming the pull of gravity and that enables the yogi to rise above a surface. In a perfectly relaxed state, such as in savasana, one may momentarily feel very peaceful and free of any constraints. Although that does not mean that the body is free of the gravitational pull. On the other hand, since this form of energy is also associated with the ease and flow of speech, it is said that mastering that energy enables the Yogi to have a smooth and clear voice. Perhaps Patanjali is referring to the feeling of lightness and ease experienced in a meditative trance, and acknowledges that contemplative thinking releases the practitioner from the hold of the material world.

Key word: Practice

The glow of health and wisdom

III.40 samana-jayat jvalanam

समान जयात् ज्वलनम् ।

samana: the vayu; jayat: by mastery; jvalanam: blazing (gastric fire)

By mastery over samana, the body-nourishing mid breath, radiance is attained.

The middle of the body life energy, the mid breath or Samana Vayu, is about nourishment and assimilation throughout the body. It helps the lungs in oxygen absorption, controls the functioning of the heart and is about the functioning and health of abdominal organs. The practitioner's digestive fire is strengthened. The mind's discriminative faculties are sharpened as she evaluates sensory and emotion related experiences. The deep meditation discipline focused on the Samana Vayu gives an aura of light around the Yogi.

Key words: Mind, Practice

The power of hearing

III.41 srotrakasayoh sambandha-samyamat divyam srotram

श्रोत्र आकाशयो: संबंध संयमात दिव्य श्रोत्रम् ।

srotra: of hearing; akasayoh: and space; sambandha: relation: samyamat: deep meditation; divyam: divine; srotram: hearing

By performing deep meditation on the relation between the sky and the ear one gets super-physical hearing.

This Sutra is about enhancing the power of the hearing sense. Thus, when the meditation is focused on the ear and the sky, the medium of air that facilitates sound movement, hearing and listening improve. A Yogi can then hear distant and even subtle sounds beyond the normal range. It is said that in a state of deep meditative absorption one can hear the divine sound 'Aum', that is deemed to be the sound of the universe vibrating. There is constant chatter going on in our minds as we are reasoning, interpreting the world, remembering or thinking about the future. There is the sense of silence, of clarity and cognition beyond that chatter. Even the degree of silence varies. There are sounds in the body that can be felt and vibrant silence in a forest that is heard. All it takes is focused attention to sense and feel all these.

Key words: Mind, Practice

<u>Body in space</u>

III.42 kayakasayoh sambandha-samyamat laghutula

samapatteh ca akasa-gamanam

काया आकाशयो: संबंध संयमात् लघू तूल समापत्ते च आकाश गमनम् ।

kaya: of the body; akasayoh: and space; sambandha: on relation; samyamat: deep meditation; laghu: light; tula: cotton; samapatteh: by merging the mind on; ca: and; akasa: space; gamanam: passage through

With deep meditation focused on the body and sky, the body and mind become light and one feels as if one can move anywhere.

The meditation discipline centered on the body, in relation to the sky, makes the body as light as cotton. It frees the seemingly solid, heavy body from the weight and confinement of thoughts and sensations and lets the mind free into the space around and beyond. This is like levitating. It is like the feeling of the body traveling great distances through space at will.

Key words: Mind, Practice

Releasing the mind

III.43 bahir-akalpita vrttih maha-videha tatah prakasavarana-
  ksayah

बहिर अकल्पिता वृत्ति: महा विदेह तत: प्रकाश आवरण क्षय: ।

bahir: external; akalpita: unimaginable; vrttih: thought;
maha: great; videha: out of the body; tatah: thence;
prakasa: of light; avarana: covering; ksayah: wasting away

The state of mind projected outside (of the body), which is not an imagined state, is called the great out-of-body (experience). By this, the covering of the light (of intelligence) is destroyed.

Centering the mind on a position outside the body can also free the mind of the hold of internal and external influences. Such meditative attention cleanses the limitations of body-based think-ing and experiencing, and all ignorance vanishes. The body cen-tered individual consciousness then frees itself of the inherent and self-created limitations on all perceptions.

Key words: Mind, Practice

Understanding the material world

III.44 sthula svarupa suksma anvaya arthavatva samyamat
  bhutajayah

स्थूल स्वरूप सूक्ष्म अन्वय अर्थवत्व संयमात् भूतजय: ।

sthula: gross state; svarupa: form; suksma: subtle;
anvaya: all-pervading; arthavatva: subservient to the
purpose; samyamat: deep meditation; bhutajayah: mastery
over the five elements

Deep meditation on the elements – their mass, forms, subtlety,
conjunction and purpose, brings mastery over all.

The deep meditative discipline yields complete information
about objects in nature; their common and differentiating qualities, as well as their functions and forms. Yet this Sutra is not
about gaining a mastery over the material world (Prakriti), but
about gaining an understanding of its true and primary function.
That function is conveying the world experience to the knower
within, the Self or our basic awareness.

Key words: Mind, Practice, Reality

<u>Understanding yields power</u>

III.45 tatah animadi pradurbhavah kayasamapat taddharma
anabhigatah ca

तत: अणिमादि प्रादुर्भाव: कायसंपत तद् धर्म अनाभिगात: च ।

tatah: from it; animadi: a siddhi; pradurbhavah:
appearance; kaya: the physical body; sampat: perfection;
tad: of them; dharma: functions; anabhighata: non-
obstruction; ca: and

Then comes the attainment of minuteness, the perfection of body
and the ability to resist the elements.

With deep meditation focused on the elements, the practitioner understands their minutest forms and functions. This en-

hances the practitioner's bodily strength and wellbeing and removes obstacles in her way and protects her from any adverse changes taking place around.

Key words: Mind, Practice

Body and mind care

III.46 rupa-lavanya bala-vajra-samhananatvani kaya sampat

रूप लावण्य बल वज्र संहननत्वानि काय संपत् ।

rupa: appearance; lavanya: beauty; bala: strength; vajra: hard; samhananatvani: firmness; kaya: body; sampat: perfection

Perfection of the body is beauty, strength, and steel-like hardness.

Proper care of the body and a peaceful mind ensure a strong and healthy body. A perfected body not only has beauty and strength, but also the ability to resist injuries and ward off any diseases.

Key words: Mind

Self-understanding

III.47 grahana-svarupa asmita anvaya arthavattva-samyamat indriya-jayah

ग्रहण स्वरूप अस्मिता अन्वय अर्थवत्व संयमात इन्द्रिय जय: ।

grahana: cognition; svarupa: own form; asmita: egoism; anvaya: connectedness; arthavattva: function; samyamat: deep meditation; indriya: senses; jayah: mastery

Deep meditation on the process of knowing, on the essence (of the sense organs), on ego, and on nature, gives control of the senses.

The meditation discipline focused on the process of perception yields insight into the senses. The senses deliver information and we assign meaning to it. We individualize that information and make sense of the world of experiences. Just as one can choose to follow the senses in search of pleasures or for keeping away from pain, they can also provide focus for turning inwards. Turning away from senses is freeing and provides control over them.

Key words: Mind, Practice

Knowledge in an instant

III.48 tatah manojavitvam vikarana-bhavah pradhan-jayah ca

तत: मनोजवि त्वंम् विकरण भाव प्रधान जय: च ।

tatah: from it; manojavitvam: speed like that of the mind; vikarana-bhavah: independent of senses;

pradhan: primary; jayah: conquest; ca: and

(With deep meditation) one gains instantaneous cognition without the use of any vehicle, like the senses, and complete mastery over Nature

The senses are the primary vehicles that connect the external world to our Self. But with the meditation discipline, by-passing the senses, one gains instant and direct understanding of and power over the senses. This in a way is gaining mastery over Nature, Prakriti, the senses being part of that.

Key words: Mind, Practice, Reality

Sutras 49-55 are about the genuine accomplishment of the ability to see things as they are and not through the conditioned lens of past experiences.

<u>Awareness and intelligence</u>

III.49 sattva-purush anyata-khyati-matrasya sarva-bhava adhisthatrtvam sarva-jnatrtvam ca

सत्व पुरुष अन्यता ख्याति मात्रस्य सर्व भाव अधिष्ठात्रुत्वं सव ज्ञात्रुत्वम् च ।

sattva: guna of illumination; purusha: individual self; anyata: distinction; khyati: awareness; matrasya: only; sarva: all; bhava: states; adhisthatrtvam: supremacy; sarva-jnatrtvam: omniscience; ca: and

Omniscience comes when one discerns the difference between the Self and the illuminative intellect.

The illuminative intelligence is part of the mind. When attained it mirrors the Self within, yet it is different from it, just as an object is different from its image in the mirror. Realization of that difference means one has overcome all the limitations due to a limited world view and biased ways of interpreting experiences. When those limitations are overcome one becomes a true observer, directly and clearly knowing and understanding the mind and everything else. One gets a complete understanding of all the evolving changes and forms around.

Key words: Mind, Self

<u>Freedom from bondage</u>

III.50 tad-varairagyat api dosa-bija-ksaye kaivalyam

तद वैराग्यात् अपि दोष बीज क्षये कैवल्यम् ।

tad-varairagyat: from non-attachment to that; api: even; dosa: defect; bija: seed; ksaye: on destruction; kaivalyam: liberation

Non-attachment to the seed of bondage and powers leads to liberation.

The various powers and abilities mentioned above can have the effect of distracting the practitioner from the true objective of Yoga, which is to find release from the limitations and sorrows that are part of worldly experiences. Therefore, it is necessary to relinquish the desire to have those powers and abilities. They stand in the way of attaining liberation and it is important to free oneself from their binding effect. What is liberation? This is the state when awareness is free of all limitations at all the times. It becomes part of every thought and action and the mind is at peace. In this state, one is free of the stresses and strains in life caused by the changing energy balances among all the interacting agencies, namely the mind and the material world. There is joy and fulfillment in life. One keeps on following routine activities, albeit with a detached attitude.

How do we, for example, liberate ourselves from the hold of the past? Alexandre Jolien's advice is: Revisit the past. What are we holding on to? Prejudices and traumas? Identifying the influences and automatic influences and automatic mechanisms that we are dragging around us, will speed us towards freedom. Revisit the past not to find excuses but to become better. [1]

Key words: Afflictions, Wisdom

1. Ricard Matthieu, Christophe Andre, and Alexandre Jollien, 2018. In Search of Wisdom: A Monk, a Philosopher, and a Psychiatrist on What Matters Most. Sounds True, Boulder, Colorado.

The lure of powers

III.51 sthany-upnimantrane sanga-smaya-akaranam punar anista-prasangat

स्थानि उपनिमन्त्रणे संग स्मय अकरणम् पुनर अनिष्ट प्रसंगात् ।

sthahny: high-placed; upnimantrane: on being invited; sanga: coming together; smaya: wonder; akarana: avoidance; punar: again; anista: undesirable; prasangat: inclination

When lured by super-physical powers, there should be neither pleasure nor pride, since undesirable connections can re-emerge.

The accomplishments and powers attained can engender vanity and distract some practitioners from staying with their objective of attaining freedom from the stresses of life. Even after attaining freedom, the lure of attaining those super powers is not completely gone. It can crop up and has the potential to draw in the attention of the practitioner. Therefore, it helps to remain on guard and withstand their pull.

Key words: Afflictions, Wisdom

Slowing time

III.52 ksana-tat-kramayoh samyamat viveka-jam jnanam

क्षण तत् क्रमयो: संयमात् विवेकजं ज्ञानम् ।

ksana: on moment; tat-kramayoh: in order; samyamat: deep meditation; viveka-jam: born of awareness of reality; jnanam: knowledge

Deep meditation on the moment, and the next, ensures discriminative knowledge.

Keeping attention focused on the moment and the next, helps strengthen the ability to comprehend reality, to wisely discriminate between alternatives, and to make appropriate choices. This is mindfulness, maintaining awareness of any experience without judgment. It stretches the time and thereby reveals the progression of unfolding events. The knowledge gained thereby is enhanced, as in slow-motion. The practitioner can see the changing and the changeless aspects of any phenomenon.

Ralph Waldo Emerson said: "To the attentive eye, each moment of the year has its own beauty, and in the same fields it beholds, every hour, a picture which was never seen before, and which shall never be seen again."

Key words: Practice, Wisdom

Observing reality

III.53 jati-laksana-desair anyata anvacchedat tulyayoh tatah pratipattih

जाति लक्षण देशैर अन्यता अन्वच्छेदात् तुल्ययो: तत: प्रतिप्रत्ति: ।

jati: class; laksana: characteristic; desa: place; anyata: otherwise; anvacchedat: undefined; tulyayoh: similar; tatah: from it: pratipattih: understanding

From knowledge comes the ability to differentiate between two objects that appear to be identical.

The ability to concentrate makes an accomplished practitioner a keen and astute observer of reality. Therefore, because of refined perception, she can notice the smallest differences in similarly placed and seemingly indistinguishable objects and appearances over time.

Key words: Practice, Wisdom

<u>Understanding reality in all its dimensions</u>

III.54 tarakam sarva-visayam sarvatha-visayam akramam ca iti viveka-jam jnanam

तारकं सर्व विषयम् सर्वथा विषयम् अक्रमम् च इति विवेकजम् ज्ञानम् ।

tarakam: transcendent; sarva: all; visayam: objects; sarvatha: in all ways; visayam: objects; akramam: successionless; ca: and; iti: finish; viveka-jam jnanam: knowledge born of the awareness of reality

Awareness of reality brings intuitive knowledge which is liberating. It includes all objects and processes, is omnipresent and omniscient and includes the past, the present and the future.

When the practitioner through intuitive understanding, understands the nature of reality, knowledge of all objects is gained. The past and the future are as clear as the present. There is no limitation or condition that stands in the way of that clarity. All phenomena reveal all details and as they are set within their contextual setting. There is freedom from all afflictions and limitations.

Key words: Wisdom

<u>The state of liberation</u>

III.55 sattva-purusayoh suddha-samye kaivalyam iti

सत्व पुरुषयो: शुद्ध साम्ये कैवल्यम् इति ।

sattva: illumination, purity; purushayoh: soul; suddha: of purity; samye: on equality; kaivalyam: liberation; iti: this

Liberation is when the purity of the intellect is equal to that of the Self or Purusha, the awareness within.

There is a form of intelligence that is balanced, unconditioned, and indicates serenity. (It is referred to earlier in Sutra III.49). It is then like the pure form of awareness. When it is attained one is liberated from the conditioning that tends to limit one's world experience. That means freedom from afflictions and a state of harmony. This state is described as self-realization, 'Kaivalya', or liberation. It is indicative of having attained the ability to distinguish between the world of experiences, Prakriti, from our inherent inborn awareness, Purusha. It enables the Yogi to understand the constant transformation that everything within and without undergoes.

Key words: Reality, Self, Wisdom

———

Chapter 6

IV. Liberation (Kaivalya)

This chapter focuses on the concepts about the two-fold nature of reality, namely the Self within us and the world that we live in. It draws the practitioner into the subtlest aspects of the mind, and highlights liberation from the hold of life's afflictions and the attainment of wisdom.

Sutra 1 is about special powers.

<u>Where do powers come from?</u>

IV.1 janma ausadhi-mantra-tapah-samadhijah siddhayah

जन्म औषधि मन्त्र तप: समाधिज: सिद्धय: ।

janma: birth; ausadhi: medicine; mantra: incantation; tapah: dedication; samadhi: total absorption; ja: born of; siddhayah: special powers

The special powers are the result of birth, medicinal plants, mantras or due to total absorption.

In the previous Chapter, there are several Sutras that mention the various special powers that can be attained through a dedicated Yoga practice. Sometimes, perhaps because of good karma earned in the previous births, one is born with those powers. Then, even dedicated practice is not needed. One can also attain powers by ingesting certain drugs, herbs and plants; which can induce fantasies. Then there are the Mantras, a few meaningful syllables or words. Words are powerful means of initiating certain states of mind and constant repetitions of those can usher in certain abilities. Or another way to attain the powers is, by subjecting the body to a rigorous physical discipline, various kinds of penance, subjecting oneself to rigors such as excessive cold or heat, or by holding uncomfortable postures such as standing on one leg. All these different ways of attaining any extraordinary powers, either using the body, substances or through perseverance, besides being temporary, bring limited success. Ingesting certain drugs can potentially cause misuse. Doing too much of any of these is also counter-productive in any endeavor. It negatively affects both the body and the mind.

The best way for attaining various mental and spiritual powers is through disciplined meditative absorption, or Samadhi; and that is the Yogic way. It addresses all aspects of living and there are no risks. The Samadhi discipline is a powerful means of understanding a wide range of phenomena and for unravelling all the mysteries of existence.

Key word: Attention, Practice, Wisdom

Sutras 2-3 are about change.

Changes come naturally and through effort

IV.2 jaty-antara-parinamah prakrty-apurat

जात्यन्तर परिणाम: प्रकृति अपूरात् ।

Jaty: kind; antara: another; parinamah: transformation; prakrty: material nature; apurat: becoming full

Transformation of any kind is the result of unfolding of natural tendencies.

Nature has abundant energy and transformative power, and that brings about changes. At the same time, any change depends on the nature of the material and the laws of nature it is subject to. Adjustments in the basic qualities of matter manifest as changes. For example, clay with water added is different from what it is when dry. Or, a plant emerging out of a seed. Just as everything exists, everything changes.

The sorrows and limiting afflictions that are part of life can also be overcome and cleared. Some may be beyond our reach and for the others relief can be found by following appropriate practices, in conformity with nature. Biological transformations may be somewhat limited but mentally there is room for endless possibilities for enhancing existential well-being. These can, as the Karma philosophy says, even extend from one life to the next.

Key words: Mind, Practice, Reality

Our choices matter in delivering change

IV.3   nimittam aprayaojakam prakrtinam varana-bhedas tu tatah ksetrikavat

निमित्तम् अप्रयोजकं प्रकृतीनाम् वरण भेदस् तु ततः क्षेत्रिकवत् ।

nimittam: incidental cause; aprayaojakam: indirectly causing; prakrtinam: of natural tendencies; varana: obstacle; bhedas: removal; tu: on the other hand; tatah: from that; ksetrikavat: like the farmer

An incidental cause does not stir up natural tendencies into activity; it merely removes the obstacles, like a farmer builds banks to irrigate his fields.

The march of change in anything continues according to natural laws and the changing balance in its inherent energies. Nature is constantly on the move responding to some instruments of change. Water keeps moving downslope until a farmer builds dams or redirects its flow. Here, the farmer is the agent who brings about the desired transformation by bringing water where it is needed.

The awareness within us remains unchanged. But when that innate awareness and nature connect, we get a limited world experience due to the shrouding of perceptions by our ignorance. To see and experience the world with clarity we need to remove any limiting conditions. Actions in themselves, good or bad, do not bring about any transformation. But they do channel the transformative process at work. Then there are other outside forces, or incidental events, that have a role to play.

Yoga practices alone do not change us, they simply remove the obstacles to our spiritual journey. Incidental occurrences do affect us, and so do the subliminal traits as they emerge to exert their influence. But mainly, it is the choices that we make and actions we opt for, that have the effect of changing the course of events in life, sometimes facilitating, and sometimes obstructing. Our choices and our ignorance about the nature of reality can affect the realization of freedom. Our future is affected by unrealized tendencies within us and by our choice between good or bad options in life. Freedom or liberation from the miseries of life is possible for all, provided we overcome ignorance and other limitations on our choices.

Key words: Mind, Practice, Reality

Sutras 4- 6 describe the nature of mind

Individualization of experiences

IV.4 nirmana-cittani asmita-matrat

निर् माण चित्तानि अस्मिता मात्रात् ।

nirmana: created; cittani: of the mind; asmita: I-am-ness; matrat: from that alone

Minds are created from a sense of being a separate 'I'.

We assign our own interpretation to any experience in life and this is the individualization of experience. The mind itself consists of first, the senses; second, the individualized impressions; and third, the intellect. All these make our overt consciousness, the created or individualized mind. This is ego, an erroneous sense of identity that limits and distorts our world experience. The impressions and the thoughts that follow this can have a limiting and distorting influence on our choices with the result that we experience pain and distress. However, if the influence of such afflicted effect is understood, it can enhance the world experience in a wholesome way. Yoga practices, through monitoring thoughts and behaviors, can be instrumental in that. We can then get a better understanding of the nature of our experiences.

Key words: Affliction (I-am ness), Mind

Awareness and mind are drivers of thoughts and actions

IV.5 pravrtti-bhede prayojakam cittam ekam anekesam

प्रवृत्ति भेदे प्रयोजकम् चित्तम् एकम् अनेकेषाम् ।

pravrtti: moving forward; bhede: difference; prayojakam: directing; cittam: mind; ekam: one; anekesam: of many

The awareness within, and not consciousness, or the created, individualized mind, is the mover of different activities and thoughts.

Our mind consists of sense directed consciousness, subtle impressions, memories, and intelligence. Their individualization results in thoughts that lead to actions. We think that thoughts and actions represent what we are. However, these do not represent our authentic identity.

Thoughts and actions are constantly evolving and shifting. They are part of nature, and are part of our manufactured, or artificial minds. Other minds also play an influential role in this and therefore the importance of teachers and close associates. All these can result in a world view that is narrow and conditioned.

If we can clear off the limitations that taint our world experiences, we can transform this built-up mind. Such transformed mind then is closer to the Self within, the energy that activates it. And that energy is our identity.

Key words: Mind, Self

Meditation for liberation

IV.6 tatra dhyanajam anasayam

तत्र ध्यानजम् अनाशयम् ।

tatra: of them; dhayana: meditation; jam: born of;
anasayam: free from impressions

Of these the mind born of meditation is free from latent impressions.

Elaborating on the first Sutra of Chapter IV, Patanjali reiterates saying that meditation is the real means for mind transformation, and not due to birth, or plants, asceticism, or mantra recitation. All latent and afflicted impressions and thoughts can be clarified through meditation. Guidance of others who have attained such ability can also be of help in attaining this. Part of the meditation discipline is learning to deal with disorienting emotions, infatuations, pride, prejudices, greed, and constant discontent. Introspection plays an important role in this. Dhyana means reflection and is about reflecting before, during and after any action and to be aware of one's thinking in all interactions. This liberates the mind from the hold of previous impressions and conditioning. Then the actions do not leave any imprints nor do they generate new Karma.

Key words: Meditation

Sutras 7- 11 focus on desire driven actions and the lessons learnt from them.

<u>Actions either bind us or free us</u>

IV.7 karma asukla akrsnam yoginah tri-vidham itaresam

कर्म अशुक्ल अकृष्णम् योगिन: त्रिविधम् इतरेषाम् ।

karma: action; asukla: not-white; akrsnam: not black; yoginah: of a yogi; tri-vidham: three-fold; itaresam: of the others

The karmas of yogis are neither white nor black, for the others they are of three kinds, white, black and gray.

Desires are beginning-less and are followed by actions. Actions that follow desires bind us, generating impressions that sustain and build up. Those impressions then draw us towards similar actions. Pleasure-giving actions motivate us to re-experience pleasure whereas pain-causing actions steer us away from those. Some impressions wait in abeyance and reactivate under appropriate conditions, in the immediate or far future. We thus tend to be bound to the cycle of opting for certain actions and re-experiencing their effects.

Actions that are virtuous and bring peace and serenity, are white. Actions that bring pain to self and others are called black and not good. There are some that are in between, neither white nor black, but gray. For example, the gray ones are actions that may energize, and help someone, but agitate or hurt others. Loud music is favored by some, and shunned by some others. Most of our actions therefore, tend to be white, black, or of a mixed nature, that is, gray.

In opting for any action motivation matters. For the accomplished Yogi who has conquered her desires, actions are neither white nor black. The reason being those actions are not generated by her own desires for pleasure or for avoiding pain. But since she acts for others, doing good or preventing bad. They do not leave any effects of any kind for her.

Key words: Afflictions

<u>Actions leave effects</u>

IV.8   tatas tad-vipaka anugunanam eva abhivyaktih vasananam

ततस् तद् विपाक अनुगुणानाम् एव अभिव्यक्ति: वासनानाम् ।

tatas: thence; tad: these impressions; vipaka: ripening; anugunanam: accordingly; eva: only; abhivyaktih: manifestation; vasananam: subliminal traits

These three types of actions leave impressions which become manifest when conditions are favorable and ripe.

This Sutra elaborates on the three types of actions; white, black, and gray mentioned in the previous one. Actions lead to desires, leave memories that build up into latent impressions ('samskara') and subliminal innate traits ('vasana') that condition us to repeat the same types of action. These acquired and innate tendencies, in turn, pull us towards the environment in which they can be satisfied. Over time a pool of such tendencies ('karmasaya') builds up that exercises its influence later. Some desires stay in the subconscious and appear under appropriate conditions. These conditions include the type of body/mind, the environment, and nature of the times. Sometimes these conditions may not be suitable and then the consequences remain dormant. Dormant desires sometimes actualize after a long gap, sometimes even in the next birth, and play a role appropriate to the type of life one is born into; as a human being, an animal, or an insect; and whether one is born into poverty or in riches.

We cannot not take any action given our need to stay alive. But by being selective and with will and effort we can opt for actions which help minimize, and even negate, certain types of adverse consequences. When actions are judiciously undertaken, they do not lead to any desires, thus leaving no imprints on the psyche. By following Yoga practices one can make skillful choices and conduct one's life appropriately.

Key words: Afflictions. Mind

Choice of actions matters

IV.9 jati-desa-kala-vyavahitanam api anantaryam smrti-samskarayoh eka-rupatvat

जाति देश काल व्यवहितानाम् अपि अनन्तर्यम् स्मृति संस्कारयो: एक रुपत्वात् ।

jati: by class; desa: by place; kala: by time; vyavahitanam: separated; api: even; anantaryam: immediate succession; smrti-samskarayoh: of memory and impressions; eka-rupatvat: because of the sameness in appearance

Memory and impressions are the same in form. They nurture tendencies that shape our lives even though their cause may be separated by class, place, or time.

Life is a continuous process for all, in all places and always. Our actions leave effects, impressions ('samskara') and memories are created and during life we have a stock of memories and their effects. There is a close relationship between memories and subliminal impressions, or 'vasanas'. A subliminal impression is the memory of an experience, unconsciously left on the mind. Some effects materialize while some remain unrealized from one life to the next, as if there were no separation between births. These can, thus, be carried over from one life to next. They can appear even if one does not have any overt memory of having experienced them before. When appropriate conditions are present some memories come back, no matter how far distant they may be in time or space and births. Those memories revitalize the previous impressions leading to certain actions. Those actions in turn leave effects, although they are not identical given the changed nature of other overall circumstances.

The consequences cannot be avoided. By being selective and avoiding actions that bring pain one can build up a pool of preferred actions. Actions that leave good imprints and bring serenity are the ones that should be undertaken without expectation of the result, success or reward. The message of the Sutra is that we can change our future through our choice of actions.

Key words: Afflictions, Mind

Freedom if desires are left unfulfilled

IV.10 tasam anadhitvam ca asisah nityatvat

तासाम् अनादित्वम् च आशिष: नित्यत्वात् ।

tasam: of them; anadhitvam: no beginning; ca: and;
asisah: of the will to live; nityatvat: eternal

Since the desire to live is eternal, there is no beginning for desires.

In life, we seek comfort and shun pain. Both these result in actions and experiences that stay in our memories. Once born, one continues seeking comfort and happiness, and each experience is motivated and affected by a previous experience.

However, if there is no desire there is no action and no effect. Not all desires are needed for survival and some can be left unfulfilled. For an accomplished practitioner who can overcome the pull of desires, there is no experience leaving any effect. It is like turning one's back to life. But that also means freedom from all the inevitable limitations and afflictions that one is otherwise subjected to. However, turning the back to life does not mean ending life, it means ending life as a conditioned experience. A desire-less person then is free to direct her life towards helping others, help them find relief from the sorrows and strains of living.

This is learning to live through action, through work and experience. It is by knowing things, enjoying things, and thus gaining experience and knowing the nature of things until the mind lets them go at last and becomes unattached. And then aiding others to attain understanding. That is the way of karma yoga in which there is no cessation of work.

For the follower of Raja Yoga nature is a means to acquire experience, and that the result of all experience is that the pure consciousness becomes aware of its separateness from nature. The conjunction with matter is continued until such realization comes.

Key words: Afflictions, Reality, Wisdom

<u>How to find freedom from the pull of desires and their effects</u>

IV.11 hetu-phala asraya alambanaih sangrhitatvad esam abhave tad-abhavah

हेतु फल आश्रय आलंबनै: संगृहीतत्वाद् एषाम अभावे तद अभाव: ।

hetu: cause; phala: effect; asraya: that which supports; alambanaih: dependent upon; sangrhitatvad: because of being bound together; esam: of these; abhave: in the absence of; tad: of them; abhavah: disappearance

Because they are bound together as cause and effect, the effects disappear with the cause.

Behind each action is a desire for something. Desires and subliminal impressions provide the impulse for experiencing pleasures in life, and they also deter us from following hurtful possibilities. We seek fulfillment through pursuing desires, finding ways of satisfying those through undertaking actions. The result is we get caught in the cycle of action and effect. Desires are unavoidable in life. But, actions undertaken to satisfy those, leave imprints in the form of subliminal urges, on our mind. The stronger those imprints become the more we are likely to repeat those same types of actions. The only way to escape recurrent cycles of actions, imprints, to actions again, is to overcome the initial motivators, the desires. Desires can, with will and restraint, be held in check; if not avoided altogether. When desires are absent, and the subliminal urges or impressions are quiet, there is no motivation to act on them, and effects, benign or painful, are not realized.

The root of all desires, subliminal impressions is our ignorance about the changeable nature of reality (avidya), and our superficial and constructed self (asmita). Once that ignorance is overcome and we become aware of our true nature, it frees us from staying caught in the cycle of wanting and satisfying.

Key words: Afflictions, Wisdom

Sutras 12-13 elucidate the evolutionary process of change. Evident is the similarity between Patanjali's and Darwin's logic, centuries apart.

Time and change as progression of shifting states

IV.12 atita anagatam svarupatah asti adhva bhedat dharmanam

अतीत अनागतं स्वरूपत: अस्ति अध्व भेदात् धर्माणाम् ।

> atita: past; anagatam: future; svarupatah: real nature;
> asti: exists; adhva: because of; bhedat: difference of
> paths; dharmanam: of properties

The existence of the past and the future in an object is as real as that in the present. The difference of properties is because of the difference of paths.

This Sutra is about time and our perceptions thereof. The past, present and the future represent reality that we think of as a continuing phenomenon. Some phenomena follow a predictable transformation given their inherent properties and due to the past affecting the present and the present the future. If they seem different, the differences are due to the differing mix of evolving properties.

In our minds too, the effects of our interactions plus our set-in tendencies manifest. The properties of all the component energies exert their own influence on how the next thought, for example, will manifest and how that in turn will affect the next. It is difficult to recognize the mix of components as they evolve through time.

Some changes are predictable, as when a seed matures into a fruit, but some are difficult to identify given the changing mix of conditions that can affect the process. We tend to consider time as something unchanging from one moment to the next, or the past as completely separated from the future; when these are simply successions of moments. The past remains within us, affecting our present, and that in turn appearing in some form in the future. Also, some elements in an object and some tendencies within us may stay dormant, or rendered unproductive, until the conditions are appropriate.

Key word: Reality

Shifting balance of properties and energies

IV.13te vyakta-sukshmah guna atmanah

ते व्यक्त सूक्ष्मा: गुण आत्मन: ।

te: they; vyakta: manifest; sukshmah: subtle;

guna: energy; atmanah: composed of

Changes in innate tendencies happen in either gross or subtle ways.

In Nature, all objects have certain inherent properties and a mix of energies ('gunas'), namely; clarity, activity, and inertia. These constitute the power behind all changes. The inherent properties and the balance among the energies of objects, become manifest in time.

Our perceptions of state of things too depend on our set-in tendencies ('samskara' and 'vasanas') and our energies manifesting at that time. The balance within all elements, both in the objects and in our mental states, keeps shifting. The previous states remain in a subtle form, they manifest in the present, and some remain latent, appearing at some later time. Essentially, the past and the future are simply different states of balance among all energies. Nothing remains the same. By staying aware of the constantly evolving changes in everything around us, and in our perceptions, we can monitor our own behaviors and choices, avoiding unwanted consequences to self and to others.

Key words: Reality

Sutras 14-24 focus on man, mind, and its subtlest aspects, and the world.

<u>Changes, perceptible and imperceptible</u>

IV.14 parinama aikatvat-vastu tattvam

परिणाम एकत्वात् वस्तु तत्वम् ।

> parinama: transformation; ekatvat: due to uniqueness;
> vastu: object; tattvam: the essence

The modifications in any object continues yet the uniqueness of the innate tendencies persists.

Objects and minds are both part of Nature. Objects around us and our perceptions thereof keep changing and the same objects may be perceived differently by different observers. The changes in objects at any time are the result of the unique combinations and balances of their innate tendencies. Yet, any object retains its specific mix of properties. For example, water gets transformed into vapor and ice, yet it remains water and not some other substance, like stone.

Our perceptions depend on our states of mind and these also keep changing. Normally it is not easy to identify the progression of any change in objects or in our thinking. Shifts in states of anything over time become noticeable to us when the mind is becalmed. We can then notice changes in perceptions along with changes in objects, all ushered in by their respective constituent energies.

Key words: Mind, Reality

Same objects, different perceptions

IV.15 vastu samye chitta bhedat tayoh vibhaktah panthah

वस्तु साम्ये चित्त भेदात् तयो: विभक्त: पन्था: ।

vastu: object; samye: being the same; chittabhedat: because of their being difference of the mind; tayo: of these two; vibhaktah: separate; panthah: path

Same objects appear different to different minds

Our perceptions of objects around us are our own. The same object is likely to be seen differently by others. Our perceiving mind keeps evolving. In any perception previous memories crop up, and we are selective in what we see and experience and interpret these in our own way.

The mind cannot change the objects through perception. The object is the same for all observers, but what one sees of any object depends on the inclinations, associations, and limitations of the perceiving entity. Yoga practices are instrumental in changing the way the mind perceives and interprets any experience. When the introspective discipline frees the mind of its limitations, it perceives the same objects clearly and therefore differently in relation to the previous perception. 'Pure seeing', perceiving in a way that is free of any bias or interpretation, can happen for one who has attained the ability to attain the state of meditative absorption.

Key words: Mind, Practice, Reality

Reality of material objects

IV.16 na cha aik-citta-tantram vastu tad-apramanakam tada

kim syat

न च एक चित्त तन्त्रं वस्तु तद् अप्रमाणकम् तदा किं स्यात् ।

na: not; ca: and; aik: one; citta: mind; tantram: dependent on; vastu: object; tat: that; apramanakam: non-cognized; tada: then; kim: what; syat: would be

The object is not dependent on any one mind alone. Otherwise what would become of it when not cognized by that mind?

This Sutra poses the question about how real the objects are. Objects are perceived by minds. Does this mean that if there are no minds around the objects cease to exist? If an object is not cognized by a mind, does it disappear for other minds? Do objects have separate and independent existence? We are selective in what we see in an object, then what happens to the part that we do not see?

According to Patanjali everything is real whether one perceives it or not. He makes the point that objects and perceiving minds are separate entities.

Key words: Mind, Reality

Perception depends on intention and attention

IV.17 tad uparaga apeksitvat cittasya vastu jnata ajnatam

तद् उपराग अपेक्षित्वात् चित्तस्य वस्तु ज्ञात अज्ञातम् ।

tad: that; uparaga: conditioning; apeksitvat: because of expectation; cittasya: for the mind; vastu: object; jnata: known; ajnatam: unknown

An object is known or unknown depending on the conditioning or expectation of the mind.

We need to connect with the objective world for survival. The senses draw us to objects which then grab our attention. How much we know about those objects depends upon the degree of our attention. When something else comes along, our attention shifts there. When the mind meets an object, any recognition thereof depends on the mind's expectation and reflection. Establishing a connection between an object and the mind is a process involving the sense organs, intelligence, and how we interpret any perception. Without these the object is not cognized.

The interactions with others also comes into play and our perception is affected by those. A conditioned mind sees an object partly and superficially, noticing certain parts and missing others. An unconditioned mind alone can know the essence of any object or experience, with clarity and entirety.

Key words: Attention, Afflictions, Mind

<u>Purusha is the seer and mind is its agent</u>

IV.18 sada jnatah citta-vrttyah tat-prabhoh purusasya aparinamitvat

सदा ज्ञाता: चित्त वृत्तय: तत्प्रभो: पुरुषस्य अपरिणामित्वात् ।

sada: always; jnata: known; citta-vrttyah: the modifications of the mind; tat-prabhoh: of its lord, purushsya: of the purusha; aparinamitvat: because of the constancy

Because of its unchanging nature, the Self or the pure consciousness always knows the permutations of the mind.

The mind by itself cannot deliver any worldly experience to us. It derives its power from our basic awareness, Purusha, the Self or pure consciousness. The mind keeps changing like any other object but the Self remains unchanged and witnesses the happenings both in the objective world and in the mind. The Self is the true 'seer' and the mind is its agent connecting it with what can be 'seen'. Existence depends on fulfilling existential needs such as hunger, thirst, shelter and sex, and others. And it is the mind that connects us with the objective world and other minds for that. And overseeing this process is the Self.

Key words: Mind, Self

<u>We are our awareness and the mind is an instrument</u>

IV.19   na tat sva abhasam drushyatvat

न तत् स्व आभासम् दृश्यत्वात् ।

na: not; tat: it; sva: self; abhasam: illuminative;

drushyatvat: because of its perceptibility

Since it (the mind) is perceptible, it is not self-illuminative.

Chitta is our mind, and the perceiving instrument, and includes the intellect. The mind itself is also an object for awareness. We experience and we are aware of different states of mind, such as anger, delight, or sadness. The mind itself is not aware of itself and its objects at the same time. When it becomes aware of some object it cannot reflect on itself at the same time. The mind is illuminated, like the moon being illuminated by the sun. Its ability to see and experience the objective world comes from the awareness within. That innate awareness, the Self, is the perceiver observing the mind. The mind is a perceived object. The awareness within sees the world around through the mind.

We think that our thoughts and beliefs represent what we are. We characterize ourselves as man/woman, young or old, or in terms of what we do, think, and possess. All these are external to what we really are, that being the Self, the awareness that sees and experiences everything.

Key words: Mind, Self

<u>Awareness observes the mind and the mind observes the world</u>

IV.20 eka-samaye ca ubhaya anavadharanam

एक समये च उभय अनावधारणम् ।

eka-samaye: at the same time; ca: and; ubhaya: both; anavadharanam: cannot comprehend

The mind cannot be both perceiver and perceived at the same time.

The mind perceives the world. We are aware of the mind perceiving the world around and that gives the impression that it is the entity doing the perceiving. Like the eye that can see things but cannot see the eye itself, the mind can perceive other things but not itself.

Then who or what perceives the mind? It is the awareness within. The mind is the object of awareness, and awareness itself is not perceived by anything else. It is awareness, the Self, observing both the mind and the mind perceiving the world. Mind cannot perceive the world as well as itself, at the same time.

Key words: Mind, Self

<u>There is only one mind in us</u>

IV.21 chitta-antara-drsye buddhi-buddher-atiprasangah smrti-samkaras ca

चित्त अन्तर दृश्ये बुद्धि बुद्धेर अति प्रसंग: स्मृति संकर: च ।

antara-drsye: our mind is not cognizable by another mind in us; buddhi-buddher: cognition of cognitions; atiprasangah: superfluity of proving too much; smrti: of memories; samkara: confusion; ca: and

There is no other mind to cognize the one mind we know. If there was such a mind, we would need another mind to cognize that one and so on. That would create confusion of memories also.

The mind is unique for each being, coordinating and organizing all the incoming information, and there are no other coexisting and competing minds within. There is also no other entity, besides the Self, the awareness, that acknowledges that mind. If there was such an entity or entities, each entity holding on to the various perceptions and memories of that mind, the result will be confusion.

Our innate awareness is the power that acknowledges what the mind (consisting of the senses, I-maker, intelligence, memories and levels of consciousness) receives, delivers and holds. The awareness simply receives and remains unaffected by what the mind delivers, like the sky and the passing clouds below.

If it were the mind overseeing its own perceptions, then the question arises that who or what oversees the mind? That would mean another entity within the mind or a chain of minds one behind the other. Again, that would be chaotic.

Key words: Mind, Self

<u>Reflection of awareness in the mind</u>

IV.22 citeh aprati samkramayah tad akara apattau sva buddhi samvedanam

चित्ते: अप्रति संक्रमाय: तद् आकार आपत्तौ स्व बुद्धि संवेदनम् ।

citeh: of the mind; apratisamkramayah: unchanging; tad: its; akara: form; appatau: on the assumption of; svabuddhi: self-cognition; samvedanam: experience

The mind knows the Self when that is reflected in the (purified) mind.

A restless mind provides a diminished, distorted, or ambiguous, impression of the world. A becalmed mind is a mind separated from the pushes and pulls of the material world. Its intelligence is free of the limitations imposed by those. The refined intelligence of the mind enables it to see and experience objectively the world as it is, in all its clarity and complexity. That intelligence makes the mind insightful, and it provides a clear reflection of what the awareness within us can receive. In such a state, it closely resembles the pure and unchanging Self within, but does not itself become that unchanging awareness. As to how to know the awareness within, it is through reaching the deepest level of meditative absorption wherein the totality of the mind is revealed.

Key words: Mind, Self

The mind delivers the world experience to the awareness within

IV.23 drastr drsya uparaktam cittam sarvartham

द्रष्टृ द्रश्य उपरक्तम् चित्तम् सर्वार्थिम् ।

drastr: the knower; drsya: and the knowable; uparaktam: colored by; cittam: the mind; sarvartham: all comprehending

The Self comprehends, both the mind, and its object that colors it.

The mind perceives objects, experiences them in various ways and makes sense of the experience and in that sense, becomes the knower. But there is another entity that knows both the mind and what it has perceived. That is the Self/awareness within (Purusha). The innate awareness becomes the knower of the mind and the material world. These two entities, the mind and awareness, are involved together in making any object, and by extension the phenomenal world, perceptible. The mind created picture of the objective world (Prakriti), with all the associated influences (memories, 'samskara', I-maker, balance of energies ('gunas')) involved therein are conveyed to the innate awareness (Purusha). Through such interaction between Purusha and Prakriti, with mind as the acting agent in-between, all knowledge becomes available.

Key words: Mind, Reality, Self

Awareness uses the mind to know the world

IV.24 tad asamkhyeya-vasanabhih citram api para artham samhatya-karitvat

तद् असंख्येय वासनाभि: चित्रम् अपि पर अर्थम् संहत्य कारित्वात् ।

tad: that; asamkhyeya: innumerable; vasanabhi: by the vasana'; citram: filled with; api: although; parartham: for the sake of another; samhatya-karitvat: due to acting in collaboration

The mind, tainted by innumerable 'vasanas', acts in collaboration with the Self.

The mind seeks connections with the objective world using the senses, memories, and provides meaning to what these bring. We think that the mind is the motivator reaching out to the world. It is, in fact, motivated by existential needs and subliminal desires ('vasana'). In this process, there are innumerable impressions that color what the mind perceives and acknowledges. However, it is not for its own sake that the mind acts to gain the world experience but it is for delivering it to the Self within (Purusha). The Self can then know the objective world.

Key words: Mind, Self

Sutras 25-34 describe what the attainment of the objective of the Yoga discipline means, namely, liberation from the hold of life's afflictions and gaining of wisdom.

<u>Realization of true identity</u>

IV.25 visesa-darsinah atma-bhava-bhavana-nivrttih

विशेष दर्शिन: आत्म भाव भावना निवृत्ति: ।

visesa: distinction; darsinah: to whom; atma-bhava: consciousness of the self; bhavana: feeling; nivrttih: complete cessation

For one who has seen the distinction between the Self and the mind, all confusion about the nature of Self disappears.

Who am I and what is the meaning of it all, are the existential questions that one comes across in life. We think that the mind is what we are. However, the mind is a constructed idea, shaped and colored by the impressions left by experiences. It is an instrument of the Self, or the real 'seer' within us. Spiritual realization means becoming aware that the mind and the 'Self' are distinct entities. That is liberation, freedom (Kaivalya), from the bondage of a conditioned instrument. With it comes wisdom which is the ability to distinguish between the real and the apparent, the obvious and authentic. The mind then is no longer deemed to be the main power behind our world experience. Our identity is not the mind but the Self within, which is pure and eternal consciousness.

Key words: Mind, Self, Wisdom

<u>Finding peace and clarity within</u>

IV.26 tada hi viveka-nimnam kaivalya-pragbharam cittam

तदा हि विवेक निम्नम् कैवल्य प्राग्भारम् चित्तम् ।

tada: then; hi: verily; viveka: discrimination; nimnam: inclined towards; kaivalya; liberation; pragbharam: gravitating towards; cittam: mind

Then the mind, with enhanced intelligence, is drawn strongly towards the seer or the Self.

The mind is drawn towards the world. But when through introspective understanding all its limitations and afflictions have been dealt with, intelligence is enhanced. This ushers in the understanding of the real nature of the world. As wisdom takes over, the mind's self-centeredness and self-indulgence are replaced by discerning intelligence. The Self which otherwise has stayed under the shroud of the world-bound mind is now free to shine and reveal the peace and clarity within itself.

Key words: Mind, Self, Wisdom

The fragility of sustained attention

IV.27 tat-chidresu pratyaya antarani samskarebhayah

तत् चिद्रेषु प्रत्यय अन्तराणि संस्कारेभ्या: ।

tat: that; chidresu: break; pratyaya: belief; antarani: interval; samskarebhayah: from impressions

Past impressions can arise and prevent the conjunction between the mind and awareness.

Past impressions tend to keep their hold on our minds. While in a state of deep concentration, they crop up and result in moments of inattention. When these impressions arise, and take hold, they distract and prevent the mind from approaching the deep awareness within us. It is only through a vigilant practice that their hold on our minds can be weakened.

Key words: Attention, Mind, Self

Overcoming distractions

IV.28 hanam esham kleshavad uktam

हानम् एषाम् क्लेषवद् उक्तम् ।

hanam: removal; esham: of these; kleshavad: like that of
the afflictions; uktam: has been described

The afflictions need to be destroyed and resolved as described
previously.

The latent impressions, when dealt with and resolved, can
be becalmed. By not responding to them and through determination they can be rendered ineffective in exercising any distracting
effect on practice. The pratiprasava and other techniques described in the earlier Sutras (for example, I.30, I.27-29, II.1-3, 10-
11, 26, and 28) are helpful in weakening and preventing dormant
impressions from becoming energized.

Key words: Attention, Practice

<u>The ultimate state of absorption</u>

IV.29 prasankhyane apy akusidasya sarvatha viveka-khyater
dharma-meghah samadhih

प्रसंख्याने अपि अकुसीदस्य सर्वथा विवेक ख्याते धर्म मेघ समाधि: ।

prasankhyane: in the knowledge of the highest meditation;
apy: even; akusidasya: free of desires and aversions;
sarvatha: in every way; viveka-khyater: discrimination
leading to awareness of reality; dharma-meghah:
showering the dharmas; samadhih: total absorption

In the samadhi called dharma-meghah, with the highest degree of
discriminative insight, there is no interest even in (the fruits) of
meditative wisdom and all the virtues.

When the highest level of meditative absorption is reached, one is free of all pain and sorrow. Discriminative insight and detachment bring wisdom. This ushers in a clear understanding of reality and reveals its true essence, and one realizes the harmony and order in everything (dharma). No longer is there a confusion between the changeable material world (Reality) and the non-material existential awareness (Self) (also see Sutras II.23, IV.12)

Key words: Practice, Reality, Self

Attainment of total freedom from suffering

IV.30 tatah klesh-karma-nivrttihi

तत: क्लेष कर्म निवृत्ति: ।

tatah: thence; klesh: afflictions; karma: action; nivrttihi: freedom

From that comes cessation of pain and freedom from the consequences of actions.

When proficiency in the highest level of absorption, referred to in the earlier Sutra, is reached, spiritual ignorance is overcome. That means understanding reality, and freedom from the hold of ego, desires, aversions and fears. Latent impressions do not get re-vitalized. Actions do not lead to consequences that cause suffering or bring about further entanglements. Whatever actions are undertaken they are for the good of others. The goal of freedom from all the sorrows and pains is reached.

Key words: Afflictions, Wisdom

<u>The whole world of experiences becomes clear</u>

IV.31 tada sarva avarana-mala apetasya jnanasya anantyaj
jneyam alpam

तदा सर्व आवरण मल अपेतस्य ज्ञानस्य अनन्त्याज् ज्ञेयम् अल्पम् ।

tada: then; sarva: all; avarana: cover; mala: impurities;
apetasya: removed; jnanasya: of knowledge; anantyaj:
because of the infinity of; jneyam: the knowable; alpam:
little

When all the impurities and obscurations are removed, little remains to be known. One gains total understanding of everything.

When the goal of Yoga is attained, all the knowledge of life
and the world opens up for the practitioner. Instead of subjective
and selective attention that limits understanding, everything is
seen in its pure and transparent nature. All the distortions, impurities and uncertainties are cleared and everything becomes
known. There are no unresolved problems, and as the real nature
of any experience is revealed, the unconditioned understanding
thereof is arrived at.

Key word: Wisdom

<u>All energies become quiescent</u>

IV.32 tatah krta arthanam parinama-krama-samaptih gunanam

तत: कृत अर्थनाम् परिणाम क्रम समासि: गुणानाम् ।

tatah: therefore; krta arthanam: having fulfilled their object;
parinama: of changes; krama: process; samapti: end;
gunanam: of the innate tendencies

When their purpose is fulfilled the process of change due to the 'gunas' comes to an end.

As mentioned before, all bodies and objects hold a mix of three energies ('gunas'); illuminative, active and resistant. In nature, every process continues unfolding, and changes represent shifting balance among these three energies. When all the afflictions have been resolved, and the practitioner has reached the ultimate level of total absorption, these energies retreat in quiescence. All the appearances of cause and effect are resolved and everything unfolds according to its innate nature. For the practitioner, the 'gunas' at this stage have fulfilled their objective of providing world experience. She has no new challenges to be faced and she is at peace.

Key word: Reality

<u>Time slows down revealing change</u>

IV.33 ksana-pratiyogi parinama aparanta-nirgrahyah kramah

क्षण प्रतियोगी परिणाम अपरान्त निर्ग्राह्य: क्रम: ।

ksana: moment; pratiyogi: corresponding; parinama: change; aparanta: end; nirgrahyah: entirely apprehensible; kramah: process

The process of change consists of moments and change becomes perceptible at the end of transformation.

Objects and our perceptions of those constantly undergo changes. Leaves change color and decay, a bud emerges and changes into a flower, happiness waxes and wanes. All such changes are due to the ongoing adjustment and readjustment of the balances within the three energies (the 'gunas'; namely, action, inertia and illumination) that are part of all objects, including our mental states. The adjustments manifest in the form of changes in appearance or function and these give the impression of movement from one moment to the next. The past becomes a collection of moments seen in the shape of forms taken, the subtle or overt changes taking place in those, and our evolving perceptions and experiences. When that flow of moments is fast, giving the impression of time passing, the movement of shifting states may not be grasped. When the flow of moments stops, the resultant changes are revealed and time seems to have come to a stop. The process is revealed and recognized at that moment. Besides revealing the true nature of things, the mind can also discern the influence of 'gunas' in bringing about changes. Meditative practices are instrumental in such slowing down the process of perception.

Key words: Reality

Separation of awareness from Nature

IV.34 purusartha-sunyanam gunanam pratiprasavah kaivalyam svarupa-pratistha va citi-sakteh iti

पुरुष अर्थ शून्यानाम् गुणानाम् प्रतिप्रसव: कैवल्यम् स्वरूप प्रतिष्ठा वा चिति शक्ते: इति ।

purusartha: four-fold aims in life; sunyanam: devoid of; gunanam: of the three innate tendencies; pratiprasavah: reabsorption; kaivalyam: liberation; svarupa: own nature; pratistha: establishment; va: or; citi-sakter: of the power of pure consciousness; iti: finis

Ultimate liberation is when the 'guna', energies, no longer serving any purpose return to their original (latent) state. And then the power of consciousness resumes its own essential nature.

When the 'guna' have reached the state of quiescence, they do not serve any purpose for the Self (Purusha). All their various manifestations in the form of emotions, thoughts and concepts dissolve and disappear in the reality that they have been part of. Everything becomes transparent for the Self. The Self (Purusha) now can function free of the mind and of the influence of 'guna'. One has attained all the objectives in life (sustenance, enjoyment, fulfillment of responsibilities, and liberation).

Freedom for the Self (Kaivalya) is separation of the Self from nature and from all the limitations and coloring that come due to connection with it. This is spiritual realization. It is the state of the fully developed consciousness. Individuality is not dis-solved, instead, it is recognized, and extended, to other beings and life. There is no motivation for the liberated practitioner to follow any desires for herself and she continues working for oth-ers. The real, essential nature of the Self (Purusha) as being eternal, conscious and blissful; is revealed to her.

Key words: Reality, Self, Wisdom

Chapter 7

Concluding Remarks

Patanjali's Yoga Sutra is primarily a practice focused document. One can see that the two major subjects of the 195 Sutras in the preceding four chapters are practice and the mind. The preponderance of Sutras (more than half of the total 195) are about the various practice options. This exemplifies the practical nature of Patanjali's Yoga philosophy. If one adds the number of Sutras that focus on attention regulation, the share of the subject of practice goes up even higher. All these Sutras provide directions regarding how to direct our movements, understand the play of inherent energies in the body, and explore into levels of consciousness, from the superficial to the subtle, within us.

Postural practice has become a part of the physical fitness culture in many parts of the world. A sustained asana practice not only means improved control over the body, it also nurtures the ability to observe and recognize messages from the body. The asana, breathing and meditation practices are based on the Indian science of health, the Ayurveda. Self-knowledge needs knowledge of the body. The number of Sutras focused on the body are not many. But through postures one can get a better understanding of not only the body but also of the mind. The body based asana and breathing practices play an important role in accessing the mind and for tuning into the pain and stress in the body and in regulating attention.

A thorough training of the body is an important part of the inward directed process of meditation, the central theme in this worldview. Therefore, the next largest chunk of Sutras goes to the subject of the mind. There are several Sutras focused on various aspects the mind. The regulation of breathing is helpful in slowing down a normally racing mind. In the beginning there are Sutras that deal with the subject of constantly moving thoughts passing through our minds. Thoughts affect how we act and thus direct the course of our lives. An understanding of our perceptions and thoughts, of the connections we have with others, of the inherent limitations on our understanding of our life experiences, can be instrumental in resetting balance in our inner and outer worlds of experiences. All these have been addressed using the calming of thoughts as the primary vehicle.

Thinking follows perception. Re-evaluating perceptions, memories, behaviors, and interpersonal relationships opens up response options. This gap between perception and response is crucial in formulating considered responses. We use the senses and signals from the body to make sense of the incoming information, and for redirecting perceptions away from the negative sensations.

The ability to hold attention is crucial for self-understanding. Patanjali therefore devotes several Sutras for that. There are several Sutras that are about how and where to direct attention, from the negative to the positive, or towards something wholesome, or peaceful. There are incremental and multi-directional changes in routine ways of incorporating all such ideas in life. Attending to thoughts nurtures patience which is very important in terms of evaluating any action. It counters reactivity. Cultivating patience, patience in acting on emotion, patience in resisting the pull of desires takes practice. Delaying gratification and channeling desires can be learnt. It helps withstand the discomfort of having to wait for gratification. Desires can be channelled into finding alternatives. That provides the energy to explore and learn. By loosening our attachment to obvious physical forms and routine mental constructs we can get an understanding of the deeper recesses of the mind. Personal experience can shape and guide our understanding.

Meditation, the art of dwelling on a sensation, idea and experience, helps slow the flow of thoughts and that provides the opportunity to examine impulses before acting on them. It helps listening. When we stay open to what is happening, what is being said, we can let go of the compulsion to respond immediately. Meditation is a disciplined practice. It strengthens the ability to concentrate at will. Feelings and passions are becalmed as troubling thoughts are kept aside. One gets a better understanding of oneself by refining attention. The skill of self-observation helps in regulating the expression of feelings. Self-understanding comes from examining our habits, how we act and react in any situation.

The next three group of Sutras focus on the limitations that color our perceptions, on the nature of the material and mental reality around us, and on the concept of our selfhood. Our perceptions, and thoughts tend to be subject to the hold of certain common afflictions. An understanding of our afflicted mind can help free us from our fears, delusions and hatreds. It fosters a life-style based on contentment that frees us from running after things and accomplishments that do not always turn out to be as fulfilling as expected. Cultivating a dispassionate stance is not difficult once one sets the mind to follow it. Such as attitude leads to more appreciation of any experience and less burnout because we do the job with intention and whole-heartedly.

The Yoga Sutras provide insight into the contemporary problem of unending stress given the pace of life in relation to the march of changes. The constant effort to cope with everyday needs and cope with changes puts a strain on the ability to manage everything. The body and mind-oriented practices are aimed at achieving and maintaining continued emotional stability. These play an important role in weakening the psychological conditioning that frequently lands us in experiencing stress. The various concepts and practices provide fruitful avenues of control for establishing balance and comfort. Those avenues are strengthened by our understanding of the mind and our actions.

There are several Sutras that address the issue of changes and highlight the complex and multifaceted nature of any occurrence. When we understand the constantly evolving nature of our world of experiences, the inevitability of movement in all aspects thereof, we can let go of the tight grasp on current situation in life. The validity of Yoga philosophy about the changing balance of innate energies in everything material, is time tested and has endured centuries of changes. The Sutras provide a realistic picture of the nature of the world we live in, which includes the multiple forces at work, their dynamism and the limited opportunities for a single participant to exercise any degree of control. This reinforces the importance of cultivating judicious ways of thinking and acting. We tend to be held captive by our own expressions of our understanding of reality. Although this need not remain so.

Regarding ethics, there are Sutras that are about positive forms of thinking and acting that enhance the quality of life for all. Patanjali provides the rationale for these in the form of ethical norms and self-disciplines that provide a wide and strong base to build life on. The ethical norms and personal disciplines address personal and interpersonal behaviors. These do not in any way present a revolutionary idea since they represent universal ethical values and are consistent with holistic thinking in general. Self-disciplines provide options in the form of self-study, dedicating oneself to a cause, separating oneself from the unclean or negative. The interlinkages between these options broaden the sphere of one's environment reducing loneliness.

The ethical norms have the advantage of minimizing disturbances in the body and the mind. They provide the moral compass needed in these times of weakening religious influence. Plus, they are valuable in terms of taking a renewed look at one's place in society. Living simply, in moderation, also facilitates social justice and does not encourage disproportionate concentration of resources in the hands of a few. Individual free choice does not always provide meaning to life. An excessive focus on individual choice and disregard of others separates one from others and that can result in loneliness.

Our idea of the nature of our self tends to be limited to the body and the sensory mind. Throughout life our bodies keep changing. Our memories stay and keep us informed about our life experiences. However, even memories change as do our values and aspirations. Yet we hold on to the idea of an unchanging selfhood. The Sutras in the very beginning point out that the observing center of awareness within us is instrumental in all our perceptions and experiences. It is unchanging and without any limits. For example, Sutra III.46 informs us that the real beauty of the body is in wellbeing and strength. Asanas make us aware of our physical limitations. Neither obsessing over the body, nor denying its urges, can bring us peace. All the thoughts, accomplishments, possessions, are like waves in the ocean.

Identity formation is an on-going process throughout life, it is shaped and affected by changing circumstances. And it is also subject to volitional influences. There are multiple levels of selfhood hidden deep in our consciousness and these are constantly undergoing the process of defining. There are unpleasant tendencies and traits hidden in the unconscious that deserve scrutiny lest they emerge and grab our minds. With practice, we can examine the conditioning influences that direct our actions. Our thoughts change us, and so do our actions. There is nothing that stays unmodified in life. Yet we hold on to the idea of an unchanging self and a constant environment. The practice of meditation can change our perceptions of self, of others, and of the world.

When we realize that there is no fixed self, and no fixed mind, it frees us to mold our 'identity' into a form that is free of all the conditioning that causes suffering. Throughout the document the Yoga Sutra has referred to the Self within us, a Self that is devoid of characteristics like likes and dislikes, a Self that is unchanging, and unaffected by the vicissitudes that are the normal part of life experiences. Our perceived identity is in fact an entity hidden under the layers of ignorance about the real. The process of Yoga is the removal of those layers and reveal our genuine self underneath. The antidote for self-centeredness is self-reflection.

When seeking to establish a sense of balance in life, a balance that is reflected in the harmony between the inner and outer worlds of experiences, a world-view based on Patanjali's Yoga Sutra provides the needed answers. Patanjali's Yoga is an impressive mental discipline and contains multiple practices for self-managing and directing one's mental forays into the ever-changing world of experiences. First-hand experience is where we find meaning for things within, not in others or in the happenings around us. All the practices are centered on a way of life that is accessible to anyone who can put in the necessary effort. All these can help provide a sense of balance and comfort for anyone.

Philosophy is a way of life. It is about our understanding of reality and has implications in terms of how we interact with others. Our understanding of the environment we live in tends to be partial and given how entangled our lives are with those of others, our understanding of our own mental environment is even more limited. We think that we have a certain degree of control over our personal environment, yet that control rapidly wanes in relation to that of others with whom we routinely interact and even less in relation to those far away. On top of that we seek a certain degree of happiness in life. Given the complexity of the web of life it is no surprise that we experience tensions, surprises and imbalances. No amount of knowledge can provide that understanding. When the multiple interconnected aspects of any experience are revealed we develop an experience-based understanding of reality.

That understanding is crucial for attaining wisdom. Wisdom is about judgment and perspective and involves the ability to communicate and cooperate with others. With the yogic way of living one attains knowledge about the body, its energies, the mind and intelligence. This provides a broad perspective regarding the experience of life and most of all, about the nature of one's true identity. We have the ability to examine our own mind, our actions and experiences and that means we can have the self-understanding to formulate and be selective in personalizing the practices that we need to follow. By learning to guide, coordinate and pull in physical, mental and interpersonal ways of moving through life we can establish an enduring peace. As the body/mind/energy resources are nurtured, a sense of balance in life returns. In this 21st century, as diverse ways of life on this planet become more interconnected and interdependent, this discipline of Yoga provides a practical and valuable worldview.

———————————

Also by Pradnya Dharmadhikari

Yoga: The Experiential Discipline

And

Questions of Faith and Reality

(A Compilation)

www.ingramcontent.com/pod-product-compliance
Lightning Source LLC
Chambersburg PA
CBHW031056250726
48655CB00004B/1470